# The
# DINNER PARTY
# COOKBOOK

# The DINNER PARTY COOKBOOK

Judith Ets-Hokin

*Illustrated by Maryanne Regal Hoburg*

**CELESTIALARTS**
*Berkeley, California*

# Acknowledgments

My *deepest appreciation to* LAUREL FEIGENBAUM *for her help and to* SANDOR BURSTEIN *for his thoughtful wine suggestions. And to my children,* REBECCA, SOLOMON, *and* GABRIEL, *for their patience.*

Copyright © 1975, 1982 by Judith Ets-Hokin

**CELESTIAL ARTS**
**P.O. Box 7327**
**Berkeley, California 94707**

Cover design by Colleen Forbes
Cover photograph by Corning Photography
Book design by Abigail Johnston
Composition by HMS Typography

First printing, February 1982
Manufacuted in the United States of America

**Library of Congress Cataloging in Publication Data**

Ets-Hokin, Judith.
    The San Francisco dinner party cookbook.

    Includes index.
    1. Dinners and dining. 2. Menus
3. Cookery. I. Title.
TX737.E87    1981    641.5'68        81-65689
ISBN 0-89087-338-0 (pbk.)        AACR2

    2   3   4   5   6   7   8   9   10        88

# CONTENTS

# Foreword

When I first married, I knew very little about cooking and entertaining. I liked to cook but I had many questions. How many people should I entertain at one time? What wines should I serve? What kinds of dishes go well together on a menu? What is the best way to serve a meal? And, most important, how could I cook dinner and be with my guests at the same time?

While I was wondering where to begin, a friend called and invited me to attend with her a series of cooking classes offered by Monsieur Paul Quiaud, chef of Ernie's Restaurant in San Francisco. It was a timely opportunity.

As I observed and worked and tasted, a new world of infinite pleasures and excitement opened to me. For several years following I attended cooking class. I gained confidence, and gradually I began entertaining close friends. Soon I was entertaining often and answering for myself those questions that had at one time so overwhelmed me.

Friends began asking me for methods and recipes. Everyone was interested in dinner party menus, especially those that could be prepared ahead. Finally a neighbor organized a group of ten people into my first cooking class. In a short time my classes grew. Soon my students began requesting additional printed menus and recipes to give to friends and relatives who could not attend classes—and that was the way the San Francisco Dinner Party Cookbook was written.

A lot has transpired in the seven years since the first publication of the San Francisco Dinner Party Cookbook. I have moved the Culinary Institute twice in search of larger quarters and at this writing we are planning another move. This time we are literally going to raise the roof to meet our current school enrollment!

The original edition of the S.F. Dinner Party Cookbook has been sold out, and I am taking this opportunity to revise the book, updating some recipes and incorporating food processor notes. In recognition of current trends I have also included several "slim" and several "nouvelle" cuisine menus for the first time.

## FOREWORD

I think you will find the menus easy and practical, as well as interesting and timely. They are all designed to help you provide the best for your guests, graciously and with ease.

# Preparing to Entertain

Entertaining people at dinner in your home is a little like creating a theatrical production. In a play, all the major elements are coordinated by the director, who makes sure the lines spoken by the actors, the set, lighting, costumes, and music are at their best and in harmony with one another—which is just the sort of coordinating the host or hostess entertaining at home must do.

Once you have chosen a date and invited a group of compatible guests, the menu must be selected, the shopping done, the wines chosen, the table set, and finally the meal prepared and served. Assuming—as almost everyone does these days—that you are to be bartender, butler, cook, and waiter, there is the necessity to plan well. The San Francisco Dinner Party Cookbook was designed to help you make your dinner party "productions" a success. How can you make sure your production will be a success?

First, if you want to have your guests seated and served at table, don't attempt more than six or eight people at a time. When selecting a menu, always consider the tastes of your guests. If there is any doubt that all of them will like kidneys, for example, it is best to choose something else.

After a menu is selected, read through the shopping list and ask yourself if all the ingredients are in season and readily available. Then read the recipes carefully. Do you have all the necessary serving and cooking utensils or reasonable substitutes at hand? Do you understand all the cooking terms and recipe instructions?

Always complete your grocery shopping at least a day in advance, leaving only highly perishable foods like fish to be purchased on the day of the party.

The evening or morning before dinner, set the table completely. Set out in the kitchen all the dishes, including the coffee cups, saucers, and serving dishes you will be using, ready to be warmed or placed on the table as needed. Check the liquor, mixes, wines, and ice. When all of this has been accomplished, prepare any recipes that require thorough chilling.

Next, do all the advance preparation possible for the rest of the meal, like chopping vegetables, shelling nuts, grating lemon peel, etc. Cover these and store in the refrigerator or on the counter top until needed.

At this point of preparation you will need approximately two hours more to finish most of the menus in this book. This may be done during the day or the two hours before your guests are due to arrive, depending upon your schedule. I do the last of the meal preparation while I'm feeding the children around five in the afternoon, finishing by seven, which leaves me time to freshen up. I rarely invite people for dinner earlier than seven-thirty.

A word about children and pets. After a brief greeting to your guests, let the children, if possible, amuse themselves in their own rooms, not in the living and dining rooms. Your guests should be relaxed and undisturbed by little cowboys and Indians, or by a child demanding a bedtime story. Put pets out of the way as well; not everyone enjoys a dog on the lap or a begging animal under the dinner table.

To save yourself from dishwashing at midnight, arrange with your own teenage child or a neighborhood girl or boy to help you that evening with the younger children, the final clearing of the table, and the dishwashing. Whenever I am unable to have that little extra help, I serve coffee in the living room and never attempt to clear the table or tidy up the kitchen while my guests are present.

At seven-thirty, I light the candles and make a last-minute check of the living and dining rooms. When my guests arrive, I am ready for them.

# Memo to the Cook

The following are certain foods or cooking terms that may need further explanation, plus some suggestions for serving.

## Butter

Without exception the butter used in the recipes throughout this book is unsalted. You may keep unsalted butter in the freezer for months (out of the freezer it turns rancid quickly), removing a portion at a time as you need it. The difference in flavor is beyond comparison.

## Coffee

Unless one or more guests prefer coffee with dinner, I serve coffee as a separate course at the end of a meal, most often in the living room. My favorite after-dinner coffee is a dark French roast, blended equally with a lighter roast. I purchase the coffee beans and then grind them as needed in a small electric grinder, using the drip method of pouring water over the blend and letting the coffee drip through a filter into a server, to be served immediately.

## Cooking Equipment

Cooking equipment is an integral part of the cooking process and should simplify and aid you in making cooking a creative and pleasurable experience. I see no reason why there should be "professional" quality cookware and a lesser-quality "home" cookware. The home cook should be able to accomplish routine tasks as quickly and easily as a restaurant chef, without concern about whether a piece of equipment will deteriorate over too high a heat or scratch if a metal utensil is used.

The following list is some of the most basic equipment that you will need to cook quickly and efficiently. It is better not to have an excessive amount of equipment. Be selective, buy gradually as you need things, and always buy the best quality available.

## A Basic Kitchen

Saucepans: 1½, 2½, 4½ qt
Stock pot: 8, 12, or 16 qt
Sauté pans: 2, 3 and 5 qt
Soup pot: 6 or 8 qt
Skillets: 8", 10", and 12"
Crêpe pan: 5"
Earthenware casseroles: 2 and 4 qt
2 earthenware open roasters,
   large and small
Heavy steel baking sheets
Mixing bowls, graduated sizes
Unlined copper egg-white bowl
Tea kettle, at least 3 qt

Large chopping board
Large pastry board
2 stainless sieves,
   fine and coarse
Food mill
De-glazing spatulas
Balloon whisk
Stainless steel sauce whisk
Rolling pin
Measuring cups and spoons
Skimming spoon
Wooden mixing spoons
Scale

*Knives*
Large chopping knife
Boning knife
Dressing steel
Long slicing knife
2 paring knives
Knife holder

*Accessories*
Kitchen scissors
Parchment paper

Twine
Cheesecloth

*Gadgets*
Apple corer
Vegetable peeler
Meat pounder
Grapefruit knife
Spring-action tongs
Hand grater
Citrus zester

Greenbean julienne
   tool
Garlic press
Pepper grinder
Nutmeg grater
Cherry/olive pitter

*Electric Appliances*
Food processor
Coffee grinder
Heavy duty mixer

# Consistency of Sauces

In the recipes following, I often write about cooking a sauce down to the "right consistency." In those instances the only way to determine whether or not a sauce is right is for the cook to look at it, perhaps put a spoon through it, and determine by its thickness or thinness whether or not it is the right consistency for that particular dish. By cooking a sauce longer, you reduce the liquid, concentrate the flavor, and thicken it (by allowing the steam to evaporate). You thin a sauce by adding liquid. A good sauce should enhance the flavor and texture of a dish and should not overpower or be overpowered by the food. A properly thickened sauce should just barely cling to the food.

# The Food Processor

In the near future, because of the invention of the electric food processor, no one will be producing hand-processed foods. Time-consuming hand-chopped vegetables, handmade pastries and breads will be rare and old-fashioned. Perhaps restaurants and food shops will charge premium prices for handmade desserts or other dishes!

In some families, the quality of cooking and eating has improved because of the food processor. Many people who have never made their own bread or pastry are now making it quite regularly. Freshly grated cheeses, freshly ground meats or nuts, thirty-second pie pastry and two-minute yeast breads are just a few examples of what can be done in the machine.

There is no need to throw away your favorite recipe books when you acquire an electric food processor; simply learn how to convert from hand to machine processing and then adapt your recipes accordingly. I have done that for you in the notes following the recipes included here.

## Food Processor Tips

The food processor does not do anything you cannot do by hand; it simply saves you a great deal of time.

The food processor is a machine without a brain. YOU are the brain and must program the machine. Once you learn the techniques for processing various foods, and how to use the discs and blades, most favorite bread and pastry recipes, slicing, shredding and chopping chores can be adapted to your machine.

Don't overprocess. Most vegetables can be chopped in less than 10 seconds, pastries finished in less than 40 seconds, and breads made in about 2 minutes.

When chopping anything, the machine must be "pulsed." DO NOT leave the machine in the ON position.

Use the steel knife to chop or purée raw and cooked fruits, vegetables, meats, nuts and cheese, and to mix pastries and batters.

Use the shredding disc to shred vegetables, fruits and cheeses.

Use the slicing disc to slice fruits, vegetables, breads, sausage, etc.

Use the plastic doughhook to knead bread dough.

The processor does not whisk egg whites or cream, grind grains, spices or coffee; nor does it slice or shred soft foods or foods too hard for the tip of a knife to be inserted.

## Hors d'Oeuvre

Each menu in this book is designed to provide a complete meal. Should you wish, however, to serve cocktails before dinner, an accompaniment is usually served.

I often serve the first course of a menu in the living room with cocktails. Should you decide to do this, be sure to announce that it is the first course of dinner, so that your guests won't "save" their appetites for later.

An alternative is a small, attractively arranged assortment of such things as pepperoncini, stuffed olives, pickled onions, tiny marinated mushrooms and artichokes, and perhaps some marinated herring. Another possibility is an arrangement of chilled raw vegetables with a bowl of sour cream or mayonnaise into which they may be dipped. All of these may be arranged hours ahead, perhaps on a partitioned dish, covered and chilled until time to serve.

Above all, it is most important not to extend your cocktail hour. A two- to three-hour cocktail period with lots of hors d'oeuvre is a meal in itself, and dinner is no longer anticipated. On the other hand, two or three hours of cocktails without hors d'oeuvre numbs the palate and consequently your guests' enjoyment of the meal.

## Keeping Food Warm

Often a recipe requires that some portion of it be kept warm while you are preparing or serving another portion of the dish. How and where to keep food warm is something you have to decide according to the arrangement of your kitchen. I have an open grill on one side of my stove that is always warm because of the pilot light.

That is where the food, sometimes lightly covered with foil, usually goes to stay warm. Sometimes the dish may remain on the stove over a still warm but turned off burner, or in a pot over hot water, or in a warm oven with the door ajar.

However, you must remember that foods with short cooking times, such as boiled vegetables and delicate grilled meats, will continue cooking while being "kept warm." You have to allow for that in the original cooking of the food, never keeping anything warm beyond 15–20 minutes. If a longer waiting time is needed, refrigerate the food or set it aside in a suitable spot and reheat just before serving.

## Reheating

I have found that most vegetables, sauces, meats, fish and poultry reheat nicely as long as the reheating time has been figured into the original cooking time. Follow the specific suggestions in each menu as to whether a rapid or slow reheating is required. Be cautious not to overcook foods when you reheat them.

## Seasonings

When preparing many of the dishes in this book, I double and sometimes triple the amount of seasonings specified. Taste is a personal matter, and my taste for highly seasoned dishes may not be yours. I have attempted to allow for this by indicating "season to taste" or "adjust seasonings" or "use 1 to 3 tablespoons."

You are the cook, so season to your own taste and let your individuality prevail.

## Service

In presenting a meal, let the type of service depend partly on the menu and partly on how many guests are expected.

If you choose a buffet-style service, by all means provide the diners with a table at which to sit. The only exception is a large buffet with a menu that does not require a knife.

Should you want a slightly more formal presentation, bring the warmed plates to the table along with the dishes to be served. This type of service requires attractive cooking/serving containers. Serve each plate yourself and ask the guests to pass them.

A third possibility is to serve from the kitchen. With hot foods, you will probably need some assistance with this type of service so that the plates can be brought to the dining room as soon as they are served.

In any case, provide small portions instead of large ones, offering second helpings if desired. No matter what kind of service you choose, make sure the plates are always warmed for hot dishes.

Don't attempt to have an absolutely formal meal where no one passes a plate or leaves the table. It is unnecessary to try to emulate the service of a luxury restaurant in your home.

## Soup Stocks and Glazes

Soup stocks are considered the foundation of cooking. A stock however, is not meant to be served as is, but is used as a braising medium to give richness and body to a dish, as a sauce base, or as a base for soups. I save all the bones and scraps of uncooked meat in plastic bags in the freezer, taking care to keep beef, veal, chicken and lamb separate. When I have an adequate amount of bones, I make stock (see page 239). Tinned stocks or broths cannot be "doctored" satisfactorily, as there is always a "canned," excessively salty aftertaste.

Glazes, sometimes called extracts, essences or concentrates, are reduced stocks which coat a spoon with a shiny layer of liquid that has been reduced down to about one-tenth of its original volume (see page 240). Glazes are unseasoned and are used in sauces, soups and braised dishes. Glazes freeze well; a brown glaze, white glaze and fish glaze should always be on hand. There is no satisfactory substitute for a glaze.

## Substitutions

The menus and recipes that follow are complete. They need no more ingredients than are specified. This does not mean that they are untouchable. According to personal taste one or two ingredients may be added or omitted with no harm done. Substituting one vegetable for another, one fruit for another, or interchanging different kinds of fish or substituting capon for chicken is the way in which new dishes are created. Substituting for preference will give you infinite variety.

You cannot, however, substitute margarine for butter, frozen or canned fruit and vegetables for fresh, or canned soups for sauces and expect results even close to those using specified ingredients.

## *"Until Done"*

The phrase "until done" refers to vegetables that are just barely tender, braised meats that are tender and browned, grilled or roasted meats that are cooked to the desired degree of doneness—for poultry, when the joints move easily, and for fish the instant the flesh turns opaque. Cakes are done when they barely begin to shrink back from the sides of the pan or when a toothpick inserted into the center of the cake comes out clean. Custards are done when a stainless-steel knife inserted into the center comes out clean.

## *Wines*

Good wine enhances the pleasure of a good dinner. Therefore it is necessary to plan the wines served with a meal as an integral part of the menu.

Any wine with a taste that is harmonious with the food it accompanies is the right wine for that food and for you. There are, nevertheless, certain traditions that are worth noting because they represent the cumulative experience of many wine drinkers of many tastes.

Generally speaking, do not serve full-bodied red wines with delicate chicken, fish, or veal dishes. By the same token, a delicate dry white wine is lost when served with a highly seasoned beef dish. If the main dish is cooked in wine, it is logical to drink more of the same wine with it.

A red wine should be in the house at least one day before it is to be served, to give it a chance to rest, and it should be opened and placed on the dinner table an hour or so before dinner. White wines should be served chilled.

Sweet wines may be served with dessert, and brandies and liqueurs are pleasant with coffee or following a meal. They complete the mood of easy, graceful elegance, but of course they are not absolutely necessary.

Specific wine suggestions accompany each of the menus in this book.

# Light Suppers

# Menu 1
## TO SERVE 6

### Crêpes Louise
with Béchamel Sauce

### Watercress and Endive Salad

### Fresh Fruit Compote

### Coconut Macaroons

WINE
*A French Vouvray*
*or a*
*Maryland White*

## Shopping List

**Fish**
¾ lb crab meat

**Produce**
2 bunches watercress
1 head endive
6 shallots
4 lb selected fruit

**Spirits**
Kirsch
Madeira wine

**Groceries**
1 lb shredded coconut
1 pt light cream

## Staples

sugar
eggs
flour

vegetable oil
Dijon mustard
tarragon vinegar
butter

salt
pepper
vanilla extract

# Menu 1

This little dinner is a perfect before- or after-theater meal. It is rich and elegant, you do not need a lot of time to consume it, and it is quick and easy to prepare as well as simple to serve. A warmed loaf of French bread and butter is a nice addition.

## Planning Ahead

Prepare the crêpes well ahead. Have the salad crisping in the refrigerator, the fruit chilling in its serving bowl. Bake the macaroons in advance and have them waiting on a serving plate. An hour or so before the guests arrive, make the crab filling, fill the crêpes, and place them in an attractive baking dish. Ten minutes before serving put them into the oven, and serve them at the table from the baking dish. A watercress and endive salad with mustard dressing is suggested.

Should you wish to serve dinner after the theater, assemble the crêpes before you go out, refrigerate them in their baking dish, then double the baking time.

# Crêpes Louise
## with Béchamel Sauce

Prepare twelve 7-inch crêpes (see Basic Recipe, page 246).

For the filling, sauté 6 finely chopped shallots in 3 tablespoons unsalted butter and add ¾ pound cooked crab meat. Add 2 beaten egg yolks and 1 tablespoon Madeira to 1½ cups béchamel sauce (see following recipe). Reserve ½ cup of the sauce and add the crab meat and shallot mixture to the remaining sauce.

Spread crêpes with the crab meat filling. Roll them and arrange on a but-

17

tered ovenproof serving dish, covering the crêpes with the reserved béchamel sauce. Cover with foil and warm in a 350-degree oven for about 10 minutes. If desired, glaze under the broiler for a few seconds just before serving.

### Food Processor Method

The crêpe batter may be combined and mixed in the bowl of the processor using the steel knife. Chop the shallots in the processor using the steel knife and short on/off strokes until shallots are finely chopped.

## Béchamel Sauce

In a saucepan melt 4 tablespoons butter, stir in 4 tablespoons flour, and cook 1 minute over a low flame, without letting the mixture take on any color. Add 1½ cups light cream little by little, until the sauce reaches the right consistency (page 6), a bit thicker than heavy cream. Season with salt and freshly ground white pepper.

# Watercress and Endive Salad

With mustard dressing. See Basic Recipes page 241.

# Fresh Fruit Compote

Select any fruit or combination of fruits, such as strawberries, raspberries, blueberries, plums, peaches, pears, apples, bananas, figs, grapes, etc. Wash the chosen fruits, drain, cut uniformly, and sweeten to taste with finely granulated sugar. Flavor with 3 to 4 tablespoons Kirsch, or any fruit brandy. Blend well, cover the dish, and let the fruit mellow in the refrigerator.

### Food Processor Method

The selected fresh fruits may be sliced in the food processor using either the 4mm or 6mm slicing disc.

# Coconut Macaroons

Beat 4 egg whites stiff. Add a teaspoon of vanilla, gradually beat in 1 cup confectioners' sugar, and continue beating until the mixture is stiff and glossy. Fold in ½ cup flour and 2 cups shredded coconut. Drop by the teaspoonful 1 inch apart on a buttered and floured baking sheet and bake at 350 degrees for 15 minutes or until brown. Yield: approximately 1½ dozen.

# Menu 2
## TO SERVE 8

Pâté Maison

Ratatouille

Quick Home-Baked Bread

Pears Stuffed with Gorgonzola Cheese

WINE
A dry Sémillon
or
one of the varietal Australian wines

# Shopping List

**Meat**
1 lb pork loin
1 lb ground pork
1 lb ground veal
¼ lb chicken livers

**Produce**
4 oz shallots
3 green peppers
1 medium eggplant
4 zucchini
5 tomatoes
8 small ripe pears

**Spirits**
Madeira wine

**Groceries**
½ pt heavy cream
2 packages dry yeast
1 qt buttermilk
small package lard
4 to 6 oz imported
   Gorgonzola
Cornichons (small
   French pickles)
½ lb walnuts

# Staples

eggs
butter
unbleached flour
   (5 cups)
sugar

olive oil
fresh parsley
garlic
onions (2)
baking powder

salt
pepper
thyme
basil
allspice

# Menu 2

If you know any pâté addicts, this unusual little supper will be well received by them. It is a very popular meal in my cooking classes, and one I share often with friends. My favorite way to serve this supper is to place the food in the center of the table after everyone has been seated, and let people help themselves. It is a lovely meal all year round.

## Planning Ahead

Every dish must be made some time in advance: the pâté a day before, the ratatouille at least 8 hours before, in order to allow the flavors to develop. In the summer the ratatouille may be served cold, and in the winter hot. Place the bread on a little board and let the guests slice it themselves. Serve tiny gherkins, as they complement the pâté, and plenty of fresh, unsalted butter with the bread. The pears may be served whole, halved, or cut into rounds.

# Pâté Maison

In a skillet over a high flame, brown 1 pound pork loin cut into 1-inch chunks in a tablespoon of clarified butter (see Basic Recipe, page 247). Season with ½ teaspoon salt, a pinch of pepper, and ½ teaspoon thyme. Remove the pork and add ¼ pound chicken livers, adding more butter if needed. Brown and season with salt and pepper. Remove the livers, turn off the flame, and add ¼ cup Madeira wine and ¼ cup finely chopped shallots. Scrape up any bits clinging to the skillet. In a large bowl place 1 pound coarsely ground pork and 1 pound finely ground veal. Season with

½ teaspoon salt, a pinch of pepper, thyme, and allspice. Add ¼ cup chopped parsley, 3 tablespoons heavy cream, and 2 eggs. Add the livers and pork chunks, the Madeira, and the shallots. Mix well. Sauté 1 table-spoon of the mixture in order to taste for seasonings. Correct accordingly. Pack into a loaf tin and place in a large pan with water approximately 1 inch deep. Cover the pâté tightly with foil and bake in a 350-degree oven for 2 hours or until the fat and juices that will have risen to the top are clear yellow. Remove the pâté from the oven and lift off the foil.

Pour off the excess fat and let cool ½ hour. Loosely cover the mold with fresh foil and place a weight on top. (I use a foil-covered brick.) Refrigerate with the weight until chilled. Unmold and slice.

### Food Processor Method

Chop the shallots in the food processor using the steel knife. The meats may be added and chopped to the desired degree of coarseness.

# Ratatouille

Heat ¼ cup olive oil in a large, heavy casserole. Add 2 thinly sliced onions and 2 cloves of garlic, cut in half. (Discard garlic before serving.) When the onions are soft, add 3 green peppers, seeded and quartered; 1 medium eggplant, peeled or not as you wish, sliced ¼ inch thick. Sprinkle salt, pepper, and basil over each layer. Cover and bring to a boil, then cook 2 minutes. Remove cover and reduce liquid, stirring occasionally. Taste for seasoning, correct, and add ½ teaspoon sugar. Cooking time depends upon how well done you like the vegetables. When finished turn off the heat and let the ratatouille stand. Serve hot, at room temperature, or chilled. Garnish with fresh parsley.

### Food Processor Method

Using the 2mm slicing disc, slice the onions. Change to the 6mm disc and slice all the other vegetables, removing them as the bowl fills.

# Quick Home-Baked Bread

This bread may be prepared with the electric mixer or food processor.

In a mixing bowl, dissolve 2 packages active dry yeast in ¾ cup warm water. Add 1¼ cups buttermilk, 2½ cups unbleached white flour, ¼ cup lard, 2 tablespoons sugar, 2 teaspoons baking powder, and 2 teaspoons salt. Blend 30 seconds on a low speed, scraping the sides and bottom of the bowl. Beat 2 minutes on a medium speed. Stir in 2 to 2½ cups more flour. Dough should remain soft and slightly sticky. Knead about 5 minutes on a generously floured board. Divide the dough into 2 parts, shape into loaves, brush with butter, put in greased loaf pans, and let rise in a warm place until double, about 1 hour. Place on the lowest rack of a 425-degree oven and bake approximately 20 to 25 minutes. Remove from the pan and cool on a wire rack.

## Food Processor Method

Mix the bread ingredients using the steel knife. When the dough is mixed, change to the dough hook, in order to knead the dough. 1 minute in the processor is equal to 5 minutes by hand.

# Pears Stuffed with Gorgonzola Cheese

Peel 8 small ripe pears and cut them in half. With a teaspoon, remove the cores and a small amount of the pulp from each half. Cream 3 tablespoons imported Gorgonzola cheese and 3 tablespoons unsalted butter together, until soft and fluffy. Fill the hollows of the pears with the cheese mixture, press the halves together, and roll the pears in coarsely chopped walnuts until coated. Work quickly to prevent the pears from turning brown. Arrange on a serving plate and chill well.

## Food Processor Method

The gorgonzola and butter can be creamed in the food processor using the steel knife.

# Menu 3
TO SERVE 6

*Sashimi*

*Oyako Domburi*

*Rice*

*Sliced Sugared Oranges*

WINE
*Hot sake or Japanese beer*

# Shopping List

**Fish**
1 lb sashimi

**Meat**
1 lb pork loin
2 whole chicken breasts

**Produce**
1 bunch celery
2 bunches green onions
½ lb mushrooms
2 green peppers
10 juice oranges

**Spirits**
Grand Marnier
Mirin wine

**Groceries**
small can wasabi
   powder
Japanese soy sauce
small bottle Chinese
   oyster sauce

# Staples

eggs (6)
chicken stock

onions (3)
vegetable oil

finely granulated sugar
short-grain rice

# Menu 3

This is an easy and quick Japanese meal. Sashimi is a firm-fleshed, fresh, raw, fileted fish, usually tuna. It is a texture food, having little more than a sweetish bland flavor. It is eaten raw, dipped into a bowl of soy sauce that has been mixed with wasabi powder, a dried and pulverized Japanese green horseradish. The domburi dish is a kind of stew, containing pork, chicken, vegetables, and egg, and is a delicious meal in itself. Ideally, chopsticks should be used for this meal.

Japanese cooking and serving utensils are available in Japanese hardware stores, and food ingredients in Japanese markets.

## Planning Ahead

The sashimi should be purchased the same day that it is to be used. Keep it well chilled, and shortly before your guests arrive, slice and arrange it attractively on small lacquered trays. Have the soy sauce and wasabi powder mixed and ready. The sashimi makes an ideal hors d'oeuvre served with drinks before dinner. Just before serving, finish preparing the domburi, being certain not to overcook the vegetables. Let the eggs set while everyone is getting settled at the table. Bring it in immediately and serve it from your wok or paella pan. The sugared oranges should be chilled well, waiting in the refrigerator. Japanese fortune cookies are a nice touch at the end of this meal.

# Sashimi

At a Japanese fish market buy a pound of sashimi, usually fresh tuna filet. Just before serving, slice the fish and arrange it on a tray. Serve with

Japanese soy sauce mixed with wasabi powder in the following amounts: ¼ cup soy sauce, 1 teaspoon or more wasabi powder. Be cautious: the horseradish is extremely piquant.

## Food Processor Method

Barely freeze the fish filet about 30 minutes in order to make the fish firm enough to slice in the processor. Use the 6mm blade.

# Oyako Domburi

Cut the following into bias strips about 1 inch long: 1 bunch of celery, leaves and all, 2 bunches of green onions, and ½ pound mushrooms. Cut 3 onions into 8 pieces each and thinly slice 2 seeded green peppers. Heat 2 tablespoons vegetable oil in a wok, paella pan, or heavy iron skillet. Add all the vegetables and allow them to cook until they begin to soften, tossing constantly with two long-handled wooden spoons, for about 1 minute. Then add 4 tablespoons Mirin wine (Japanese wine) and 1 tablespoon bottled Chinese oyster sauce. Remove from the heat. In another pan, heat 1 teaspoon vegetable oil and add 1 pound pork loin and 2 whole skinned, boned chicken breasts, both cut into thin strips. Cook the chicken and pork only until they change color, about 5 minutes, and then add the meats to the vegetables. This much may be done well ahead. Just before serving cook the whole mixture over a brisk flame, stirring now and then until the vegetables are tender but still crisp, about 1 minute. Then add 6 well-beaten eggs, pouring the eggs over the vegetables and meat in a spiral so as to cover them completely. Do not stir mixture after adding the eggs. Let the eggs set, about 5 minutes, over a low flame and serve immediately.

## Food Processor Method

All the vegetables should be placed in the feed tube at an angle in order to produce diagonal slices. The chicken breasts and pork loin may be slightly frozen (about 30 minutes) so that they are stiff enough to slice neatly. Use the 4mm disc for all.

# Rice

Using short-grain rice, follow the directions on the package, substituting chicken stock for water.

# Sliced Sugared Oranges

Use approximately 1½ juice oranges per guest. With a sharp paring knife, peel and seed the oranges, being certain also to cut away the white membrane under the peel. Slice the oranges into thin rounds and sprinkle liberally with finely granulated sugar and 2 or 3 tablespoons Grand Marnier. Chill until ready to serve.

## *Food Processor Method*

Using the 6 mm slicing disc, apply gentle pressure while slicing the peeled oranges.

# Menu 4
TO SERVE 4

## Stacked Crêpes and Ham
with Mornay Sauce

## Sliced Herbed Tomatoes

## Peaches in Caramel Sauce

WINE
*French Muscadet, California Sylvaner,*
*or a German May Wine, in season.*

## Shopping List

**Meat**
1 lb boiled ham

**Produce**
3 tomatoes
4 firm ripe peaches

*Spirits*
Madeira wine

**Groceries**
2 oz imported Gruyère
2 oz parmesan cheese
½ pt heavy cream

## Staples

milk
eggs
butter

flour
sugar
olive oil

red wine vinegar
fresh parsley
fresh or dried basil

# Menu 4

This is an informal, rich little supper that is fun to make for four or six friends on, say, a Sunday evening. Provided all the ingredients, including the crêpes, are at hand, this simple meal may be prepared in about half an hour.

## Planning Ahead

Assemble the stacked crêpes ready for the oven, prepare the tomatoes and allow to marinate. The sauce for the peaches may be prepared with the peaches added but not heated. Fifteen minutes before serving, put the assembled crêpes in the oven. The peaches may be warmed just before serving.

# Stacked Crêpes and Ham
## with Mornay Sauce

Make sixteen 5-inch crêpes (Basic Recipes, page 246) and set aside. Prepare 2 cups of Mornay sauce (see following recipe) and set aside. Bring to room temperature 1 pound good-quality boiled ham. Slice the ham into 12 slices approximately the same diameter as the crêpes. Butter a large flat ovenproof casserole. Place 4 crêpes side by side on the bottom of the dish and cover each crêpe with a slice of ham. Spread some of the Mornay sauce over the ham and then cover with another crêpe. Continue stacking, ending with a crêpe on the top. Spoon a generous amount of sauce over each stack. When ready to serve, place in a 350-degree oven until hot and bubbling, about 10 minutes.

### Food Processor Method

The crepe batter may be combined and mixed in the bowl of the processor using the steel knife. If your processor has an expanded feed tube the ham and tomatoes may be sliced in the machine, using the 2 mm slicing disc for the ham and the 6 mm disc for the tomatoes.

## Mornay Sauce

In a heavy saucepan, melt 4 tablespoons butter and blend in 4 tablespoons flour. Stir until smooth and cook for a few minutes. Stirring constantly, blend in 1½ to 2 cups hot milk. Continue to stir until the sauce thickens slightly. Blend 1 teaspoon Dijon mustard, 2 oz freshly grated gruyère cheese, 2 oz freshly grated parmesan cheese, and 2 oz heavy cream. Continue to stir over a low heat until smooth.

# Sliced Herbed Tomatoes

Slice 3 firm, ripe, peeled tomatoes thinly and evenly. Arrange in overlapping slices on a platter. Sprinkle with salt, freshly ground pepper, a pinch of sugar, and lots of minced fresh or dried basil. Drizzle with olive oil and red wine vinegar. Sprinkle with 2 tablespoons minced parsley. Let stand at least 30 minutes.

# Peaches in Caramel Sauce

Peel and halve 4 fresh peaches. In a heavy skillet, melt ¼ pound unsalted butter, add ¾ cup sugar, and melt, stirring constantly with a wire whisk, over a low flame. Add approximately ½ cup Madeira wine, continuing to stir. When the sauce is smooth, add the peach halves. Turn over several times, spooning the syrup over them, allowing them to warm. Serve in individual glass dishes with plenty of the caramel sauce. Pass a bowl of whipped cream.

## To Peel Peaches

Drop the peaches into rapidly boiling water for 20 seconds. Remove peaches and peel immediately or later, just before using. If they are to stand peeled for more than 5 minutes, put them into a bowl of lemon juice and water so that the outside will not discolor.

# Hearty Dinners

# Menu 5
## TO SERVE 8

## Potage Bonne Femme
Cream of Leek and Potato Soup

## Coq au Vin
Chicken in Red Wine

## Butter Lettuce and Parsley Salad

## Petits Pois à la Française
Peas French Style

## Hazelnut Meringue Cake
with Apricot Cream Filling

WINE
*The wine you cook with.*
*This is one meal for which you*
*do not serve white wine with fowl.*
*For dessert, Angelica or a tawny Port.*

# Shopping List

**Poultry**
4-lb capon

**Produce**
6 leeks
24 tiny white onions
small head butter
   lettuce
2 lb fresh green peas

**Spirits**
good-quality red
   burgundy wine
brandy

**Groceries**
½ lb hazelnuts/
   filberts
4-oz package dried
   apricots
1 pt heavy cream

## Staples

potatoes (4)
milk (1 qt)
eggs (6)
bacon
garlic
flour

parsley
butter
sugar, granulated and
   powdered
white vinegar
lemon

salt
cayenne pepper
bouquet garni
chervil
vanilla extract

# Menu 5

This is a French meal that includes both a classic soup and a classic chicken dish. Cream of leek and potato soup is a soup in its own right as well as a base for many other French soups. Chicken cooked in red wine is a dish that every serious cook should know how to make. The hazelnut meringue cake is my favorite cake in the book.

## Planning Ahead

Bake the cake in advance, keeping the filling separate and refrigerated. Assemble the cake an hour or so before your guests arrive. Everything else may be made well ahead, and reheated before serving. Be careful not to overcook the chicken as you re-heat it. A butter lettuce and parsley salad may be served after the chicken.

# Potage Bonne Femme
## Cream of Leek and Potato Soup

Melt 2 tablespoons butter in a soup pot. Add 4 medium potatoes, finely sliced, and the white parts of 6 leeks, washed thoroughly and shredded. Reserve the green of one leek for garnishing. Season with salt and cayenne pepper and stir over a slow fire until the vegetables are softened. Add 4 cups milk and stir over a medium fire until it comes to a boil. Simmer, covered, for 20 minutes. Put the mixture through a sieve or a food mill. Return the soup to the pot, add 3 egg yolks beaten with 1 cup heavy cream, and thicken over a slow fire, stirring constantly. When ready to serve, reheat and add more cream if it is too thick. Garnish each bowl with the finely shredded green of the leek.

### Food Processor Method

Using the 2 mm slicing disc, slice the potatoes and leeks. (Do not attempt to purée the potatoes in the processor.)

# Coq au Vin
## Chicken in Red Wine

Blanch 4 slices of bacon cut into pieces with 24 tiny peeled* white onions in boiling water for 30 seconds. Drain well. Brown a cut-up 4-pound capon in 2 tablespoons butter, remove, and then brown the bacon and onions in the same pot. Return the chicken to the pot, pour ½ cup warmed brandy over the chicken, and flame. Add enough good-quality red burgundy wine to come about ¼ of the way up the sides of the pot. Add a clove of crushed garlic and a bouquet garni (see page 247). Cover and cook in the oven at 350 degrees or on top of the stove for about 30 minutes or until done. When the chicken is tender, remove to a serving dish to keep warm, remove the bouquet garni from the liquid, and thicken the wine sauce slightly with a beurre manié (see page 247), starting with a piece the size of a pea and adding more if needed. The sauce should be thin, thickened just enough to barely cling to the chicken. Adjust the seasoning. Sprinkle with chopped parsley when ready to serve.

*Be sure not to cut off root end of onion.

# Petits Pois à la Française
## Peas French Style

Put 2 tablespoons butter in a saucepan and add 8 leaves of butter lettuce, shredded, ½ teaspoon salt, 1½ teaspoons sugar, 1 tablespoon chopped parsley, and ½ teaspoon chervil. Add 2 generous cups freshly shelled peas, mix all together, and finish cooking until barely tender, using the green vegetable method (page 242), adding not more than ½ cup boiling water. There should only be a tablespoon or so of water left in the pot. If desired, a small piece of beurre manié (see page 247) may be added. Return the pan to the fire, shaking it to roll the peas around until the butter-flour mixture has combined with the liquid.

# Butter Lettuce and Parsley Salad

See Basic Recipes on page 241.

# Hazelnut Meringue Cake
## *with Apricot Cream Filling*

Whisk 4 egg whites until stiff, then beat in gradually, 1 tablespoon at a time, a cup of finely granulated sugar. Continue beating until very stiff, adding 1 teaspoon vanilla and ½ teaspoon vinegar. Last, fold in 5 ounces toasted (in the oven for 5 minutes at 350 degrees), ground hazelnuts (8 ounces of nuts with shells are roughly 5 ounces shelled). Pour into two 8-inch greased and floured cake tins and bake 30 to 40 minutes in a 375-degree oven, until delicately browned.

If hazelnuts (sometimes called filberts) are not available, substitute toasted, ground walnuts. Nuts may be ground quickly in the blender or nut grinder and spread on a metal tray to toast in the oven.

## *Food Processor Method*

The hazelnuts may be ground in the food processor using the steel knife, and the cooked apricots purée very nicely using the steel knife.

## Apricot Cream Filling

Soak 4 ounces dried apricots overnight in a little water, add 4 tablespoons sugar and the juice from half a lemon; cover, and simmer gently until soft enough to sieve. Whip 1 cup heavy cream with 2 tablespoons powdered sugar. Carefully fold in the sieved or puréed apricots. Spread the apricot-flavored cream generously on the bottom layer of the cake. Add the top layer and sprinkle with powdered sugar. Any additional apricot cream may be served on the side.

# Menu 6
## TO SERVE 8

## Velouté de Tomates à la Provençale
Tomato Soup Country Style

## Navarin des Quatre Saisons
Braised Lamb and Potatoes

## Romaine Salad

## Pear and Banana Tart

WINE
*Serve the same wine you cook with*
*or a Sauvignon Blanc, or,*
*from France, a Montrachet.*

## Shopping List

**Meat**
1 lb bacon
4 lb cut-up lamb,
    shoulder or leg

**Produce**
2½ lb ripe tomatoes
1 small white cabbage
2 leeks
4 ripe pears
4 ripe bananas
2 heads romaine lettuce

**Spirits**
light sauterne wine
dry white wine

## Staples

eggs
butter (½ lb)
flour
sugar
vegetable oil
parsley
garlic

onions
potatoes (2½ lb)
chicken stock (4 cups)
rice
red wine vinegar
apricot jam

salt
pepper
thyme
basil
bay leaf
white pepper

# Menu 6

This is a hearty French provincial-style meal, with an unusual tomato soup that is thickened with rice. The lamb is highly seasoned with garlic, and the pear and banana tart is my own combination. This is an easy dinner to prepare and serve.

## Planning Ahead

Finish preparing the soup in advance and reheat before serving. The lamb and potatoes can be finished ahead and kept warm or reheated. The tart may be prepared ahead but not baked until the guests arrive so that you may serve it warm. I use a paella pan to cook the potatoes, and present the dish at the table in the paella pan, lamb over the potatoes, garnished with parsley.

# Velouté de Tomates á la Provençale
*Tomato Soup Country Style*

Sauté 10 minced slices of bacon in a heavy skillet. Discard all but 2 tablespoons of fat and add 2 chopped onions and 2 chopped leeks, white parts only. Sauté gently for about 5 minutes. Peel and seed 2½ pounds ripe tomatoes and mash into the pan with the bacon, onions, and leeks. Sauté for 10 minutes more. Add ½ cup light sauterne wine and 1½ cups chicken stock. Discard the tough outer leaves of a small young cabbage and finely mince the heart. Add to the tomato mixture. Season with salt and pepper, 1½ teaspoons dried basil, 1 teaspoon dried thyme, and 1 teaspoon sugar. Simmer gently, uncovered, for 40 minutes. Meanwhile, cook ⅓ cup rice until it is soft and mushy. Combine, batch by batch in an electric blender, the soup, rice, and 2 peeled cloves of garlic. (Garlic is optional.) Purée briefly so that the soup does not become too smooth. Return the soup to the pot, add ½ cup more sauterne and ½ cup water and simmer gently, covered, for 30 minutes. Adjust seasoning. If it is not thick enough, simmer uncovered until it reduces to the right consistency. Serve very hot.

### Food Processor Method

Mince the chilled bacon in the processor using the steel knife, remove and chop the onions and leeks. Remove and finely chop the cabbage. The food processor may be used to purée the soup—also using the steel knife.

# Navarin des Quatre Saisons
### Braised Lamb and Potatoes

Heat 4 tablespoons clarified butter (see page 247) in a heavy casserole and quickly brown 4 pounds cubed lamb over a high flame. Pour off the excess fat and add 3 or more cloves of crushed garlic, 2 tablespoons flour, 1 teaspoon thyme, 1 bay leaf, 4 tablespoons chopped parsley, 1½ cups dry white wine, and ½ cup chicken stock. Season with salt and white pepper and cook covered over a moderate heat for 20 minutes or to the desired degree of doneness. Remove the meat to be kept warm, and reduce the liquid. Check the seasoning and, if desired, strain the sauce.

## Potatoes

Melt 4 tablespoons butter in a large open casserole or paella pan. Add 2½ pounds peeled potatoes cut into small cubes, sprinkle with salt, white pepper, and enough chicken stock to just cover the potatoes. Place in a 425-degree oven and bake until the stock is cooked away. Serve the lamb over the potatoes, pour the sauce over the lamb, and garnish each plate with minced parsley.

# Romaine Salad

See Basic Recipes page 241.

# Pear and Banana Tart

Prepare a tart pastry (see Basic Recipe, page 244), chill, and roll out to about ⅛ inch thickness. Shape into an 8-inch tart tin. Dot the pastry with bits of unsalted butter, sprinkle with sugar, and add 1 layer each of thinly sliced, peeled pears and bananas. Sprinkle each new layer with sugar and dot with butter. Place the tart on the floor of a 425-degree preheated gas oven for 10 minutes or over the coils on top of an electric stove for 7 minutes, in order to brown the lower crust. Finish baking on the rack of a 350-degree oven for about 10 minutes more, or until the crust is nicely browned. Glaze with sieved apricot jam.

## Food Processor Method

Both the pears and bananas may be sliced in the processor using the 4 mm slicing disc.

# Menu 7

## TO SERVE 8

Cold Cream of Cucumber Soup

Veal Ragout

Noodles with Butter and Parsley

Lemon Cake

WINE
With the soup, an Italian Verdicchio or
a California Pinot Blanc;
for the veal, Valpolicella from Italy or
a California Zinfandel.

## Shopping List

**Meat**
2½ lb veal shoulder

**Produce**
4 cucumbers
2 large tomatoes
2 green peppers

**Groceries**
1 lb (fresh if possible)
  egg noodles
1 doz ladyfingers
1 can sweetened
  condensed milk
½ pt heavy cream

## Staples

milk
eggs (4)
butter
flour
cream of tartar

fresh parsley
onions (2)
lemons (4)
chicken stock
salt

pepper
sweet Hungarian
  paprika
caraway seeds
  (optional)

# Menu 7

This is a good summer menu and one that has been my favorite meal to travel with. The lemon cake is a popular one; when served partially frozen, it has a texture similar to cheesecake. This menu can quite easily be adapted to serve 12 or 14 people at a buffet.

## Planning Ahead

Have the cucumber soup well chilled and on the table when your guests sit down. Forty minutes before serving, put the room-temperature veal into a preheated oven, being careful not to overcook it. The pasta holds nicely on top of the stove, ready to be tossed with butter and parsley just before serving.

## Planning Ahead for Travel

Finish the cucumber soup the day before and chill in a covered plastic container. The lemon cake should be baked and frozen the day before as well. In the morning brown and completely assemble the veal ragout so that it can be put into the oven whenever you are ready. The soup and cake go into the ice chest and hours later arrive still chilled.

# Cold Cream of Cucumber Soup

Peel, cut in half lengthwise, scoop out the seeds, and slice 4 large cucumbers. Cook in 2 tablespoons butter over low heat about 10 minutes. Stir in 3 tablespoons flour and gradually add 2 cups chicken stock, stirring constantly. Add 1 cup of milk scalded with 4 thin slices of onion. Simmer slowly for 15 minutes. Put the soup in the blender and purée. Stir in ½ to 1 cup heavy cream, depending upon the thickness of the soup, season with salt and white pepper, and chill. This soup is lovely served in glass bowls and garnished with a thin slice of scored cucumber.

### Food Processor Method

The cucumber and onion may be sliced using the 2 mm slicing disc. Using the steel knife, purée the soup.

# Veal Ragout

Cut 2½ pounds veal shoulder into small cubes. Brown the meat quickly in hot clarified butter (see page 247) in a heavy pan. Remove the meat and add 1 finely chopped large onion. Cook slowly, until the onion is lightly browned. Return the meat to the pan and add 2 tablespoons sweet paprika, 2 teaspoons salt, ½ teaspoon sugar, 2 large tomatoes cut into eighths, 2 medium-sized green peppers, seeded and cut into small pieces, and 1 tablespoon caraway seeds (optional). About 40 minutes before serving, cover and place in a preheated 375-degree oven. Stir occasionally to prevent scorching.

### Food Processor Method

Chop the onion in the processor using the steel knife.

# Noodles with Butter and Parsley

Cook 1 pound wide egg noodles in lots of boiling, salted water until barely tender. Drain, return to the pot, and toss with ¼ pound unsalted butter and 3 tablespoons fresh, minced parsley. Add salt and white pepper to taste. Keep warm or reheat and serve with the veal.

### Food Processor Method

The parsley may be minced using the steel knife.

# Lemon Cake

Lightly butter a 7-inch springform pan. Line the bottom and sides of the pan with ladyfingers. Blend thoroughly 1 can sweetened, condensed milk with 4 egg yolks, 1 teaspoon freshly grated lemon zest* and the juice of 3 large or 4 small lemons. Beat the 4 egg whites with ½ teaspoon cream of tartar until stiff, and fold into the lemon mixture. Pour the batter into the pan and bake in a 375-degree oven until the top is nicely browned, about 20 to 30 minutes. Put into the freezer until ready to serve.

*Citrus zest is the outer or colored part of the rind.

### Food Processor Method

The milk, egg yolks, lemon zest and juice may be combined in the processor using the steel knife.

# Menu 8
## TO SERVE 8

*Ceviche*

*Paella Valenciana*

*Garlic Toast*

*Romaine Salad*

*Strawberries with Cream*

WINE
*California Barbera or a Spanish Rioja.*
*For dessert, Lagrima from Málaga*
*or a California Gold Muscatel.*

## Shopping List

**Fish**
1 lb firm white fish
  filet (halibut, red
  snapper, etc.)
2 dozen clams
2 dozen mussels
2 fresh lobster tails

**Poultry**
3-lb chicken

**Produce**
1 bunch fresh cilantro
  (Chinese parsley)
7 limes
2 heads romaine lettuce
3 pts ripe strawberries

**Meat**
2 or 3 Chorizo or
  other highly spiced
  sausages

**Groceries**
small can chopped
  Mexican green chilies
3 small cans pimientos
½ pt heavy cream
loaf of French bread

**Spirits**
Kirsch

## Staples

butter
sugar
olive oil
vegetable oil
garlic

onions
chicken stock (4 cups)
rice (2 cups)
red wine vinegar
vanilla extract

salt
pepper
saffron

# Menu 8

This is a menu containing two classically Spanish dishes you might be served in any part of Spain. Ceviche, always made with a firm-fleshed regional white fish, is a marinated raw fish salad. The lime juice marinates and "cooks" the fish. The distinguishing ingredients of paella are saffron, rice, chicken, and shellfish—the shellfish varying greatly according to the region. A paella pan is an important part of the presentation and one should be used. Since the paella contains shellfish, poultry, meat, rice, and vegetables, no side dishes are needed.

## Planning Ahead

The ceviche should marinate 5 or 6 hours before serving and makes a good hors d'oeuvre with cocktails. Finish the paella to the point of its last baking, putting it into the oven 25 minutes before serving, adding the seafood the last 4 or 5 minutes. Don't overcook it, as the paella tends to get dry. Crisp garlic toast is a nice accompaniment to the paella, with a romaine salad following. Berries for dessert make a simple end to this meal. The paella in its pan is such a beautiful dish it should always be served at the table.

# Ceviche

Cut 1 pound of a boned and skinned firm white fish, such as halibut, into small pieces. Put them into a deep china, pottery, or glass dish. Add half a small onion finely chopped, 3 tablespoons finely chopped cilantro (Chinese parsley), and chopped green chilies to taste. Pour ¾ cup fresh lime juice and 2 tablespoons olive oil over the mixture and let marinate at least 4 or 5 hours in the refrigerator.

## Food Processor Method

The onions, cilantro and chilies all may be chopped in the processor, using the steel knife.

# Paella Valenciana

In a paella pan sauté a cut-up 3-pound chicken in ½ cup foaming butter to which 2 cloves of crushed garlic have been added. When the chicken is golden brown, remove and set aside. In the juices remaining sauté 2 cups rice until golden. Add ¼ teaspoon saffron, or more to taste, and 4 cups chicken stock and bring the liquid to a boil. Season with salt and pepper. Cook the rice uncovered over a low flame for 20 minutes. Now add the chicken pieces with 2 or 3 sliced Chorizo sausages (or any spiced sausage) and ¾ cup diced pimientos. With a large cooking spoon mix the chicken, rice, sausage, and pimiento together. This much may be prepared well ahead. When ready, bake in a preheated 350-degree oven uncovered for approximately 20 to 25 minutes. Add more chicken stock if needed. Add large shelled shrimp, clams, and mussels in their shells, and shelled lobster tails and cook until the clams open and the shellfish is red, about 4 or 5 minutes more. Serve from the paella pan and be sure that each guest gets some of everything in the dish.

# Garlic Toast

Soften 4 ounces unsalted butter and blend thoroughly with 2 crushed cloves of garlic. Cut a loaf of French bread in half lengthwise. Cover generously with the garlic-butter, sprinkle with salt and put into a 400-degree oven for 7 or 8 minutes, until golden and crisp. Slice and serve immediately.

*Food Processor Method*

Using the steel knife, the butter and garlic may be creamed in the processor.

# Romaine Salad

See Basic Recipes, page 241.

# Strawberries with Cream

In a saucepan combine ¼ cup sugar and ¼ cup water. Bring the mixture to a boil, and simmer 5 minutes. Add 2 tablespoons Kirsch and pour over 3 pints cleaned and hulled ripe strawberries. Chill. Serve with whipped cream that has been sweetened with powdered sugar and flavored with a few drops of vanilla extract.

# Menu 9
## TO SERVE 6

Marinated Sweet Peppers

Ground Meat Loaf with Tomato Sauce

Purée de Pommes de Terre aux Fines Herbes
Puréed Herbed Potatoes

Pots de Crème à la Vanille
Individual Vanilla Custards

WINE
Grenache or Gamay Rosé

## Shopping List

**Meat**
1 lb ground lean beef
½ lb ground pork loin
½ lb ground veal

**Produce**
8 sweet peppers
fresh chives (optional)

**Groceries**
sliced white bread
1 can tomato purée
1 large can Italian-type
  tomatoes
1 small can tomato
  paste
1 pt heavy cream
1 pt light cream

## Staples

milk
butter
sugar
olive oil

fresh parsley
onions
potatoes (2 lb)
mayonnaise
lemons
red wine vinegar

salt
pepper
chervil
tarragon
basil
vanilla extract

# Menu 9

Whenever I announce this menu to my classes, a few people say they need not come to me to learn how to prepare meat loaf and mashed potatoes. On the other hand, there are those who enjoy cooking a family dinner, and I count it as one of my favorites. It makes a perfect Sunday afternoon meal, when families with children often get together. The cold meat loaf makes delicious sandwiches.

## Planning Ahead

The pots de crème may be prepared in the morning and placed in the refrigerator to chill. The peppers should marinate 2 or 3 hours and are delicious served with cocktails before dinner. The meat loaf may be finished baking a half hour before serving and allowed to rest in a warm place until ready to slice. The mashed potatoes wait very nicely in their pot on top of the stove for reheating or, if they are to be served for a buffet, can be kept in a covered serving dish in a warm oven.

# Marinated Sweet Peppers

Char 8 sweet green (and red, if possible) peppers over an open flame and remove the skin. Cut into strips and marinate in the vinegar and oil dressing on page 241, adding 2 whole cloves of garlic and 1 tablespoon or more of minced parsley to the marinade. Discard the garlic before serving. Serve with buttered french bread.

## Food Processor Method

The marinating sauce may be mixed in the food processor. In the bowl with the steel knife, mince the parsley, then add the oil and vinegar. etc.

# Ground Meat Loaf with Tomato Sauce

Place 1 pound ground beef, ½ pound ground veal, and ½ pound ground pork in a large bowl. In the electric blender place 4 slices white bread that have been soaked in milk and then squeezed dry. Add salt, black pepper, an onion cut into pieces, 2 tablespoons tomato purée, and 3 to 5 tablespoons mayonnaise, depending upon how moist you prefer the loaf. Run the blender on low speed until everything is chopped and well-mixed. Add the ingredients to the meat in the bowl, and mix thoroughly with your hands. Correct the seasoning, pack the loaf into a well-greased loaf pan, and bake 60 minutes in a preheated 375-degree oven. When it is done remove the loaf from the oven, pour off any accumulated fat, and allow it to rest at least 20 minutes before slicing. Serve with tomato sauce, page 245.

## Food Processor Method

All the meats may be ground in the food processor using the steel knife. Remove the meats and add the bread, seasonings, onion, tomato purée and mayonnaise. Process a few seconds until well blended and add mixture to the meat.

The tomatoes may be chopped in the processor, using the steel knife.

# Purée de Pommes de Terre aux Fines Herbes
### Puréed Herbed Potatoes

Boil 2 pounds peeled, quartered potatoes until soft but not mushy. Drain and put through a sieve or food mill and return the purée to the pan. Add salt and pepper to taste, 4 or more tablespoons unsalted butter, and gradually stir in enough light cream to obtain the desired consistency, blending over a very low flame. Add all or any combination of the following herbs: chopped parsley, chives, chervil, tarragon. Start by adding a teaspoon, tasting, and adding more if desired.

### Food Processor Method

All the herbs may be chopped in the processor using the steel knife. (Do not attempt to purée the potatoes in the food processor.)

# Pots de Crème à la Vanille
*Individual Vanilla Custards*

Warm 2 cups heavy cream with 2 teaspoons vanilla extract and ½ cup sugar. Remove from heat and add 6 beaten egg yolks, stirring constantly. Strain the mixture through a fine sieve into small custard pots. Set the pots in a pan of water, cover, and bake in a 325-degree oven for about 15 minutes, or until done. Serve well chilled.

# Menu 10
TO SERVE 8

## Zuppa de Vongole
Fresh Clam Soup

## Lingua de Bue Brasata
Beef Tongue Braised in Red Wine

## Pommes de Terre Mont Rouge
Potato-Carrot Purée

## Granite
Fruit-Flavored Ices

WINE
*Unless you use a superb wine to braise with,*
*drink a different one—*
*a robust California Cabernet Sauvignon*
*or any Beaujolais red.*

# Shopping List

**Meat**
4 lb fresh beef tongue

**Produce**
8 medium-sized carrots
5 lb tomatoes
1 bunch celery

**Groceries**
1 small can clam nectar
1 pint light cream

**Shellfish**
2 to 4 dozen fresh clams

**For Ices**
5 lemons
7 oranges
2 pt strawberries

**Spirits**
dry white wine
dry red wine

# Staples

olive oil
garlic
parsley
onions

butter
eggs
sugar
potatoes (6)

cloves
bay leaf
Dijon mustard
salt
white pepper

# Menu 10

It has been my experience that many Americans have never tasted tongue. Beef tongue is a tender, succulent, tasty meat, and an economical cut besides. The shape is what most people object to, and once the tongue is sliced, the original shape is hard to imagine. After all the protest in my classes over cooking and eating tongue, everyone agreed it was absolutely delicious. Any cut of braising beef may be substituted for the tongue on this menu; simply eliminate the preboiling step. I always serve the delicious clam soup in large white soup bowls. The red soup and the white bowls make a striking combination.

## Planning Ahead

Everything must be prepared well in advance. Begin the ices at least 6 hours ahead of time. The tongue may be removed from the pot when done, sliced, placed on a serving platter, covered and kept warm or re-heated. Finish preparing the sauce and reheat it before serving. Finish the potatoes and reheat them. Prepare the soup just before your guests arrive, leaving the tomato sauce and clams separate. Reheat the tomato sauce before pouring it over the steamed clams.

# Zuppa de Vongole
*Fresh Clam Soup*

Heat 6 tablespoons olive oil in a heavy deep saucepan. Add 2 crushed cloves of garlic and cook, stirring over a moderate heat for about 30 seconds. Pour in 1 cup dry white wine, add 5 pounds ripe tomatoes that have been peeled, seeded, and coarsely chopped, and bring to a boil.

73

Reduce the heat and simmer the sauce, partially covered, for 10 minutes. Scrub 2 to 4 dozen clams, depending upon how many clams you wish to serve each guest, and drop them into a heavy skillet containing about ⅛ inch of boiling bottled clam juice or water. Cover tightly and steam the clams over a high heat for 5 minutes, until they open. Strain all the clam juice in the skillet through a cloth into the simmering tomato sauce. The soup can wait at this point. Just before serving, transfer the clams to large heated soup plates and reheat the tomato sauce for a minute or two. Pour it over the clams, and sprinkle with chopped parsley.

### Food Processor Method

The tomatoes may be chopped in the processor using the steel knife.

# Lingua de Bue Brasata
## Beef Tongue Braised in Red Wine

In a large pot, cover a 4-pound fresh beef tongue with cold water. Add an onion stuck with cloves, bring to a boil, cover, reduce the heat, and simmer for 2 hours. Remove the tongue from the pot and reserve the liquid. When the tongue is cool enough, remove the skin and cut away the fat, bones, and gristle at its base. Preheat the oven to 350 degrees. In a heavy flameproof casserole heat 1 tablespoon olive oil and brown the tongue on both sides. Remove the tongue and add 1 cup finely chopped onions, ½ cup finely chopped carrots, and ½ cup finely chopped, peeled celery. Cook the vegetables over moderate heat, stirring frequently, until they are softened and lightly browned. Pour in ¾ cup dry red wine and boil briskly for a minute. Place the tongue on top of the vegetables, add 2 cups of the tongue stock (just barely cover the tongue), ¼ cup chopped parsley, and half a bay leaf. Bring to a simmer, cover, and place in the oven for approximately 1½ hours, or until the tongue is tender. Let the tongue rest 20 minutes and slice thinly. Strain the braising liquid and boil until the sauce thickens slightly, or put the vegetables through a food mill and return them to the liquid to make a thicker sauce. Reheat the sauce when ready to serve, and spoon it over the tongue slices.

*Food Processor Method*

Chop the onions, carrots, celery and parsley in the processor using the steel knife. The sauce from the tongue may be puréed in the processor using the steel knife.

# Pommes de Terre Mont Rouge
*Potato-Carrot Purée*

Cook separately in boiling salted water 6 potatoes and 8 medium-sized carrots. Drain the vegetables and put them through a fine sieve. Beat into the combined carrots and potatoes 1 to 2 cups light cream, 1 egg yolk, and ¼ pound unsalted butter. Season with 1 teaspoon Dijon mustard, salt, and white pepper to taste.

# Granite
*Fruit-Flavored Ices*

The following amounts make about 1½ pints of each flavor.

| *Lemon Ice* | *Orange Ice* | *Strawberry Ice* |
|---|---|---|
| 2 cups water | 2 cups water | 1 cup water |
| 1 cup sugar | ¾ cup sugar | ½ cup sugar |
| 1 cup fresh lemon juice | 1 cup fresh orange juice | 2 cups puréed fresh berries |
| | juice of 1 lemon | 2 tablespoons fresh lemon juice |

In a 2-quart saucepan, bring the water and sugar to a boil over moderate heat. Timing from the moment the sugar and water begin to boil, let the mixture keep boiling for exactly 5 minutes. Immediately remove the pan from the heat and let the syrup cool. Stir in the fruit juices or purée. Pour the mixture into a shallow dish or pie pan and freeze. Stir with a fork every 30 minutes or so, scraping into the mixture the ice particles that form around the edges. The finished ice should have a fine, snowy texture. Serve in champagne glasses.

# Menu 11
TO SERVE 8

Eilene's Portuguese Seafood Stew

Rice with Peas

Garlic Toast

Butter Lettuce and Parsley Salad with Cheeses

Rich Chocolate Cake

WINE
Either Portuguese Vinho Verde
or California Pinot Chardonnay

## Shopping List

**Fish**
2 lb red snapper or
   any other firm white
   fish filets
1 lb raw shrimp

*Spirits*
dry white wine

*Produce*
1 bunch carrots
1 large green pepper
4 ripe tomatoes
2 lb fresh peas
2 heads butter lettuce

*Groceries*
several salad cheeses
1 quart buttermilk
small can unsweetened
   cocoa
3 ounces semisweet
   chocolate
½ pint heavy cream
1 loaf French bread

## Staples

olive oil
butter
onions
garlic
beef stock (1 cup)
chicken stock
   (3½ cups)

sugar
light brown sugar
parsley
rice (1½ cups)
vegetable oil
wine vinegar
flour
baking soda
eggs

fresh or dried basil
paprika
salt
pepper
vanilla extract

# Menu 11

My friend Eilene brought this sensational recipe back from a recent visit to her family in Portugal. I have gotten nothing but raves from the people in my classes for this dish. The quick and easy cake is the chocolate cake most preferred by my children and friends. This meal is deliciously filling and informal and one of my favorites.

## Planning Ahead

The stew without the fish should be made in the morning and left all day to increase the flavors. Four or five minutes before serving, add the fish and shrimp and reheat, being careful not to overcook the seafood. Gently reheat the rice and peas and turn into attractive serving dishes. Serve at the table in large white soup bowls, if you have them. Place the fish on top of the rice and serve plenty of garlic toast. A separate butter lettuce salad course, served at the table with one or two cheeses, is suggested.

# Eilene's Portuguese Seafood Stew

In a large deep pot heat 1 tablespoon olive oil and 1 tablespoon butter. Add 1 large, chopped onion, and a clove of minced garlic. When the onion is softened, add 1 large green pepper, seeded and chopped, 1 large carrot, chopped, and 4 medium tomatoes, peeled and chopped. Stir together and add 1 cup beef stock, ½ cup dry white wine, ½ teaspoon sugar, 1 teaspoon or more of fresh or dried chopped basil, ½ teaspoon or more of paprika, and salt and pepper to taste. Bring the mixture to a boil, then reduce the heat and simmer for 15 minutes. Just before serving, add

2 pounds cubed red snapper filets (or any firm white fish filets) and simmer 1 minute. Then add 1 pound shelled and deveined raw shrimp and cook until they turn pink—about 30 seconds. Garnish each serving with chopped parsley and serve in large soup bowls over rice with peas.

## Food Processor Method

Using the steel knife, you may chop the onion, garlic, green pepper, carrot and tomatoes in the processor.

# Rice with Peas

Bring to a boil 3⅓ cups chicken stock and water. Add 1½ cups long-grain rice and cook about 15 minutes. Then add approximately 2 cups fresh peas, 3 tablespoons butter, and salt to taste, and cook until the rice and peas are done, about 10 minutes more.

# Garlic Toast

Soften 4 ounces unsalted butter and blend thoroughly with 2 crushed cloves of garlic. Cut a loaf of French bread in half lengthwise. Cover generously with the garlic butter, sprinkle with salt, and put into a 400-degree oven for 7 or 8 minutes, until golden and crisp. Slice and serve immediately.

## Food Processor Method

With the steel knife, mince the garlic, then add the butter, and process until well creamed.

# Butter Lettuce and Parsley Salad

See Basic Recipes, page 241. Serve with one or two of your favorite cheeses.

# Rich Chocolate Cake

If possible, make this cake in an electric mixer. In a large mixing bowl combine 1⅔ cups flour, 1½ cups sugar, 1 cup unsweetened cocoa, 1½ teaspoons baking soda, 1 teaspoon salt, 4 ounces unsalted butter, 1½ cups buttermilk, 1 teaspoon vanilla, and 2 eggs. Blend on a low speed 30 seconds, scraping sides and bottom of the bowl. Beat 3 minutes on medium speed. Pour into two 8-inch layer pans that have been greased and floured. Bake in a preheated 350-degree oven 30 to 35 minutes, or until done. When finished baking, turn out onto racks to cool. Frost between layers and on top as desired (see following recipe).

## Food Processor Method

The cake ingredients may be mixed in the processor using the steel knife.

# Icing

In a heavy saucepan, melt 6 tablespoons unsalted butter, add 3 ounces semisweet chocolate and melt, stirring constantly. Add 1 cup light brown sugar and ¾ cup heavy cream. Bring to a boil, and boil about 3 minutes, or until thick enough to spread. Cool slightly before spreading.

# Menu 12
## TO SERVE 8

*Swiss Fondue*

*Entrecôte, Shallot Sauce*

*Potatoes in Cream*

*Romaine Lettuce Salad*

*Lemon Tart*

WINE
*A first-quality Bordeaux Red or
California Cabernet Sauvignon*

## Shopping List

**Meat**
8 ½-inch-thick
  entrecôtes (market,
  rib eye, or any
  favorite steak cut)

**Produce**
12 shallots
2 bunches romaine

**Spirits**
dry white wine
Kirsch

**Groceries**
1 lb imported Swiss
  cheese
1 loaf French bread
½ pint heavy cream

## Staples

garlic
milk
butter
parsley
potatoes (4 large)
flour

eggs
granulated sugar
powdered sugar
lemons (2 large)
arrowroot
vegetable oil

red wine vinegar
Dijon mustard
salt
pepper
fresh or dried
  oregano

# Menu 12

Nearly everyone likes steak, so when I invite finicky eaters for dinner, this is my safe menu. The fondue makes a wonderful hors d'oeuvre or first course. It is enjoyable for your guests to watch it being made as well as fun to eat. The entrecôte, with its shallot sauce, is an interesting way to serve steak, and the lemon tart is rich and light at the same time.

## Planning Ahead

Prepare the fondue either in the living room to be served as an hors d'oeuvre or at the dining table for the first course. Be sure to have all the ingredients at hand when you are making it. Time the potatoes to be done when you are ready to eat. Grill the steaks and finish preparing the shallot sauce ahead of time. When ready to serve, reheat the sauce and coat the steaks. The lemon tart may be served at room temperature or chilled. A romaine salad is recommended.

# Swiss Fondue

Rub the inside of an earthenware casserole with a clove of garlic, then discard garlic. Place the casserole over a fondue burner or a chafing-dish rack. Add 1 cup dry white wine and heat. Add 1 pound grated imported* Swiss cheese. Heat the mixture, stirring constantly until the cheese is melted and well-blended with the wine. Add 1 teaspoon or more Dijon mustard and 2 tablespoons flour mixed to a paste with a little water. Stir

*Do not use domestic Swiss cheese as it may curdle.

in 2 tablespoons Kirsch. This dish is eaten directly from the casserole, which should be kept warm over a low flame. Should the fondue thicken too much, stir in a little more Kirsch. The guests spear torn pieces of French bread with their forks and dip them into the fondue.

### Food Processor Method

Using the medium grating disc, you may grate the cheese in the processor.

# Entrecôte, Shallot Sauce

Select 8 thin (½-inch-thick) rib eye steaks. Sprinkle with salt and pepper and fry quickly in a little butter in a heavy skillet over high heat to the desired degree of doneness (one-half minute each side for rare). Remove from the pan to a serving platter. Over medium heat, add 4 tablespoons butter to the pan juices, and sauté 12 finely minced shallots, 4 tablespoons or more finely minced parsley, and 1 tablespoon or more dried oregano. Continue cooking gently over the heat until most of the liquid has cooked away. When ready to serve, coat each steak thickly with the resulting sauce.

### Food Processor Method

The shallots and parsley may be chopped in the processor, using the steel knife.

# Potatoes in Cream

Peel 4 large potatoes and slice them in rounds about ¼ inch thick. Put the slices in a heavy skillet, season with nutmeg, a pinch of salt, and lots of freshly ground pepper. Pour in a cup of milk and simmer uncovered for 15 minutes, turning the potatoes often. Rub the inside of an earthenware casserole with butter, and put the potatoes in. Pour in a cup of heavy cream, dot the top with butter, cover, and place in a 300-degree oven for about 2 hours, or until the cream is absorbed and potatoes are soft. Check the seasoning and brown the surface under the broiler. Serve hot.

## Food Processor Method

The potatoes may be sliced using the 6mm slicing disc.

# Romaine Lettuce Salad

See Basic Recipes, page 241.

# Lemon Tart

Make the tart pastry on page 244, chill, roll out to ⅛-inch thickness, and line an 8-inch buttered tart pan with a removable bottom. Grate the zest (outer yellow peel) of 2 large fresh lemons. Put 2 eggs and 3 yolks in a mixing bowl. With a wire whisk, beat in ½ cup confectioners' sugar until smooth. Beat in the juice from the 2 lemons, the grated zest, and 2 teaspoons arrowroot that has been blended with 2 tablespoons milk, and 6 tablespoons melted butter. Fill the tart shell, and place the tart on the floor of a 425-degree preheated gas oven for 10 minutes, or over the coils on top of an electric stove for 7 minutes, to brown the bottom crust. Finish baking on the rack of a 350-degree oven for 15 minutes more.

## Food Processor Method

Make the pastry in the processor using the steel knife (see page 7). The eggs and sugar may be processed with the steel knife, then with the machine running add the lemon juice, zest, arrowroot and butter — process until well blended.

# Menu 13

TO SERVE 8

Lamb Curry

Rice with Peas and Onions

Yoghurt Salad

Romaine Lettuce Salad

Mango and Pistachio Mousse

WINE
Offer beer for those who like it with curry,
or a Chianti from Italy or California.
With dessert,
a California Moscato Amabile.

# Shopping List

## Meat
3½ lb boned lamb,
  shoulder or leg
½ lb thinly sliced
  bacon

## Produce
1 bunch celery
1 green pepper
2 to 3 lb fresh
  green peas
3 large cucumbers
3 tomatoes
1 Bermuda onion
2 heads romaine lettuce
3 ripe mangoes

## Groceries
5-oz can coconut juice
1 pt plain yoghurt
8 oz shelled peanuts
8-oz package raisins
8-oz package shredded
  coconut
4 oz shelled pistachio
  nuts
½ pt heavy cream
mango chutney

## Staples

butter
onions (4)
garlic
flour
chicken stock
  (5 cups)
rice

eggs
sugar
vegetable oil
red wine vinegar
curry powder
ground ginger
ground turmeric

ground cardamom
ground coriander
cayenne pepper
salt
pepper
paprika
dry hot mustard

# Menu 13

One of the menu requests that I get repeatedly from students is for curry. Every cook should know how to prepare at least one good curry. Also, from the cook's point of view, curry is a very easy meal to prepare and serve, and one that is ideal for a large buffet.

## Planning Ahead

Make the curry well ahead, and reheat when ready to serve. The rice waits very nicely to be reheated slowly. Have all the condiments on the table before the guests sit down. For a condiment server, I use small individual porcelain ramekins on a natural straw tray. It looks pretty and works perfectly. The yoghurt salad is served with the curry, on a small separate plate. I add hot dry mustard to the oil and vinegar dressing for the romaine salad. The mango and pistachio mousse is a delicate and unusual end to this exotic meal.

# Lamb Curry

Brown 3½ pounds cubed lamb, shoulder or leg, in 2 tablespoons clarified butter (see page 247). Remove the meat, lower the flame, and add 3 medium onions, coarsely chopped, 2 peeled stalks of coarsely chopped celery, a coarsely chopped green pepper, and 2 crushed cloves of garlic. Cook the vegetables until they are soft. In a small bowl mix together 4 tablespoons commercial curry powder, 1 teaspoon each of ground ginger and turmeric, and ½ teaspoon each of ground paprika, cardamom, coriander, and cayenne pepper, 2 tablespoons flour, ½ teaspoon salt, and 2 turns of the pepper grinder. Add half of this mixture to the vegetables and allow to cook for a minute or so. Add 5 ounces canned coconut juice, 10 ounces chicken stock, and 4 to 6 tablespoons plain yoghurt. Stir until the sauce boils and then taste it. Add more of the mixed spices until the curry is to your liking. Return the meat to the pan and cook, covered, until tender. Serve over rice with peas and onions and with the following condiments: chutney, crumbled bacon, coarsely chopped onions, chopped peanuts, raisins, and grated coconut.

*Food Processor Method*

Using the steel knife, chop the onions, celery, green pepper and garlic.

# Rice with Peas and Onions

In 3 tablespoons unsalted butter, sauté a large chopped onion until it is softened. Add 3½ cups chicken stock; bring to a boil and add 1½ cups rice. Cook about 15 minutes, then add 2 to 3 cups fresh green peas. Cook until the peas and rice are done, correct the seasoning, and serve.

*Food Processor Method*

Chop the onion in the processor, using the steel knife.

# Yoghurt Salad

Peel, seed and chop coarsely 3 cucumbers and 3 tomatoes. Add 2 tablespoons coarsely chopped red Bermuda onions and mix with plain yoghurt, one spoonful at a time, until the yoghurt nicely coats the vegetables. Salt and pepper to taste and refrigerate until ready to serve.

*Food Processor Method*

The cucumbers, tomatoes and onion may be chopped in the processor using the steel knife. These vegetables should be coarsely chopped, probably 3 or 4 rapid on/off movements.

# Romaine Lettuce Salad

See Basic Recipes, page 241. Add hot, dry mustard to taste to the oil and red wine vinegar dressing.

# Mango and Pistachio Mousse

Peel and slice 3 very ripe mangoes. (A drained 8-ounce can of mangoes may be substituted if the fresh are unavailable.) Purée in the blender and put through a fine sieve to remove the fibers. Return to the blender and add ¼ cup shelled pistachio nuts and blend another few seconds. Add ½ cup melted unsalted butter and blend a moment more. In a large bowl beat together 1 whole egg and 3 egg yolks, add ⅓ cup sugar and continue beating until mixture is thick and creamy. Mix mango and egg mixture together, then carefully fold 1 cup stiffly whipped cream and 3 stiffly whisked egg whites into the mixture. Pour into individual dishes. Chill at least 5 hours.

## Food Processor Method

The processor may be used instead of the blender in the following order: With the steel knife, purée the mangos and pass through a food mill or fine sieve. With the steel knife, finely chop the nuts, and with the machine running add the butter, the eggs and sugar, processing until the mixture is thick and creamy. The whisking of the egg whites and cream and the folding process must be done by hand.

# Menu 14

TO SERVE 8

## Soupe à l'Oseille
Sorrel Soup

## Boeuf à la Mode Marseillaise
Pot Roast of Beef Marseilles

## Grilled Tomatoes

## Crème Renversée au Caramel
Caramel Custard

WINE
French Châteauneuf-du-Pape or California Barenblut.
With dessert, a French Haute Sauterne or a
Sweet Sauvignon Blanc,
"Château type," from California

## Shopping List

### Meat
1 lb salt pork
4- to 5-lb beef pot
   roast, cross rib,
   sirloin, etc.

### Produce
4 bunches sorrel
4 carrots
8 medium-sized ripe
   tomatoes

### Groceries
1 pt heavy cream

### Deli
8 oz fresh black olives
8 oz fresh green olives

### Spirits
dry blackberry brandy

## Staples

milk
butter
chicken stock
   (4 cups)
eggs (8)
onions

garlic
parsley
tomato paste
beef stock
sugar
potatoes (4)

cracked peppercorns
coarse salt
bay leaves
thyme
vanilla bean or
   vanilla extract

# Menu 14

This is another dinner from the French provinces. The sorrel soup, with its tart lemony flavor, makes a refreshing beginning to the meal. The secret of the unusual pot roast is the use of a dry fruit brandy (do not use a sweet liqueur) to give the meat and sauce a delicate, vaguely fruity touch. Be certain not to use canned olives, but the Greek or Italian type preserved in brine or oil. Hot French bread with butter goes well with this meal.

## Planning Ahead

Prepare the pot roast well ahead and slice it thinly on the diagonal. Reheat and arrange the slices on a platter when ready to serve. Finish making the sauce and have the olives and pork cubes waiting to be added as a garnish. Put the tomatoes on a baking sheet, ready to go into the oven when the soup is served. Finish preparing the soup to the point marked in the recipe, reheating and adding final ingredients just before serving. The custard must be well chilled before it is turned out of the mold.

# Soupe à l'Oseille
*Sorrel Soup*

Wash 4 bunches sorrel and remove coarse root ends. In a large heavy soup pot, melt 4 tablespoons unsalted butter. Add the sorrel and toss until all the leaves are well-coated and softened. Add 4 peeled and thinly sliced potatoes and 4 cups chicken stock. Bring to a gentle boil and simmer, covered for about 25 minutes. While cooking, mash the potatoes a bit with a fork to thicken the soup. Season to taste with salt and pepper.

This much may be done ahead. Just before serving, reheat the soup and carefully add, stirring constantly, 3 egg yolks beaten with ½ cup heavy cream.

### Food Processor Method
Using the 2mm slicing disc, slice the potatoes in the processor.

# Boeuf à la Mode Marseillaise
*Pot Roast of Beef Marseilles*

Cut 12 long larding strips from a pound of salt pork and soak them in 1 cup dry blackberry brandy. Cut the rest of the pork in large dice and fry until crisp. Remove and drain on paper towels. Pour 3 tablespoons of the pork fat into a large heavy casserole. Lard a 4-pound beef sirloin, or any favorite braising cut of beef, with the blackberry-marinated salt pork lardoons, saving the brandy. Sprinkle with coarse salt and cracked black pepper, and brown quickly on all sides in the hot pork fat. Remove the roast; add 2 onions coarsely chopped, and 3 or more minced cloves of garlic, and sauté lightly. Place the browned beef on its vegetable bed and add 3 bay leaves, a dozen sprigs of parsley, and 2 to 3 teaspoons of dried thyme. Stir 3 tablespoons tomato paste into the reserved brandy and pour over the beef along with enough beef stock to just cover. Bring to a boil over high heat, and place covered in a 350-degree oven for approximately 2 hours, depending upon how well-done you like the meat. Lift out the beef and keep warm. Skim off the fat and boil the vegetables 5 minutes over a high heat to draw out the final juices. Strain the liquid into a smaller pot and continue boiling to reduce and concentrate the flavors. Taste for seasoning. Sauté 8 ounces each of both green and black fresh, whole, unpitted Greek or Italian olives in 2 tablespoons of butter for 2 minutes. Slice the meat diagonally, cover with sauce, and garnish with olives and crisp fried pork cubes.

*Food Processor Method*

The onions, carrots and garlic may be chopped in the processor using the steel knife.

# Grilled Tomatoes

Slice off the tops of 8 medium-sized firm, ripe tomatoes. Sprinkle with salt, pepper, and a little sugar. Dot each with butter and bake in a 400-degree oven for about 10 minutes.

# Crème Renversée au Caramel
*Caramel Custard*

Warm 1 cup heavy cream and 1 cup milk with a vanilla bean or 1 teaspoon vanilla extract. Beat together 3 eggs, 2 egg yolks, and ½ cup sugar until well-blended. Remove the vanilla bean from the hot milk and gradually pour the milk into the egg mixture, stirring constantly. Heat 1 cup sugar in a heavy skillet over moderate heat until it is melted. Gradually add ½ cup water and boil until well-blended and brown. Pour the caramel into a ring mold, turning the mold around and around until the entire inside is well-coated. When the caramel is set, pour the custard into the mold and set the mold in a pan of hot water. Bake in a moderate oven for about 45 minutes, or until set. Cool and chill. When well-chilled, unmold onto a serving dish.

# Menu 15
## TO SERVE 8

Lemon Soup

Moussaka à la Turque

French Bread Toast

Salad with Feta Cheese

Melon in Season

WINE
Minos (a Cretan wine) or a California Riesling.

## Shopping List

**Meat**
2 lb freshly ground
 lamb shoulder

**Produce**
3 medium eggplants
2 large tomatoes
2 heads of romaine
 lettuce
melon in season

**Groceries**
½ pt heavy cream
1 can tomato paste
1 large can Italian
 tomatoes
¼ lb Greek feta cheese
loaf French bread

## Staples

lemons (3)
rice
eggs (6)
chicken stock
 (6 cups)
butter

onions
garlic
parsley
flour
vegetable oil

sugar
red wine vinegar
basil
salt
pepper

# Menu 15

This moussaka is another "meal in one"—meat, vegetables, and eggs. It may be prepared as much as a day in advance, refrigerated, and then baked just before serving. Prepared in a charlotte mold and garnished with parsley, it resembles a Turkish fez when it is turned out. It is easy and impressive to serve. The lemon soup is classically Mideastern and in keeping with the rest of the menu.

## Planning Ahead

The last guest's arrival signals the time to put the room-temperature moussaka into the oven. When it has finished cooking, let it stand in a warm place while you serve the soup. After the soup is finished and the dishes cleared away, turn the moussaka out onto a large platter, garnish with parsley to resemble the tassle on a fez, and surround it with hot tomato sauce. Bring it to the table and serve, cut like a cake, with tomato sauce spooned over each serving. A romaine salad with Greek feta cheese, either in the salad or on the side, is the next course. Sliced melon which has been chilling in the refrigerator for at least 2 hours finishes the meal.

# Lemon Soup

Add ⅓ cup rice slowly to 6 cups boiling chicken stock and cook covered until the rice is very soft. Whisk the yolks of 4 eggs with the juice of 2 large lemons, beating them well. Just before serving add ¾ cup heavy cream to the stock and bring to a boil. Pour a little of the hot broth into the lemon-egg mixture, stirring constantly. Remove the soup from the heat and when it has stopped boiling, stir in the egg-lemon mixture. Continue to stir the soup for a few seconds and serve immediately. Garnish with a small piece of lemon peel.

# Moussaka à la Turque

Place 3 eggplants in boiling water for 20 minutes to soften all sides of the eggplant skin. Cut the eggplants into quarters lengthwise and remove the meat, reserving the skins. Chop the eggplant pulp finely and set aside. In a large, deep pot heat 2 tablespoons butter. Add 2 finely chopped onions and a finely chopped clove of garlic. When the onion is softened, increase the heat and add 2 pounds freshly ground lamb shoulder and brown lightly. Then add the chopped eggplant and 2 peeled, seeded, and chopped tomatoes and continue cooking 5 more minutes. Season with 2 or more tablespoons finely chopped parsley, 1 tablespoon chopped basil, salt, and pepper to taste. Add up to 3 tablespoons flour, stirring until the moisture is nearly all absorbed, then add 2 beaten eggs. Oil the sides and bottom of a charlotte mold and line it with the eggplant skins in such a way that they may be later folded over the filling, purple side out. Fill the prepared mold with the meat-vegetable mixture and fold the skins around it so that they meet at the top if possible. If you are not going to bake the moussaka immediately, put it into the refrigerator until an hour or so before baking. When ready to bake, place the mold in a larger pan of hot water and bake at 375 degrees for 45 minutes, or until firm. Remove from the oven and allow it to stand 20 minutes, then unmold it onto a heated platter. Surround the moussaka with a rich tomato sauce, garnish with parsley, and serve.

## *Food Processor Method*

With the steel knife, chop the eggplant, the onions, the garlic, the tomatoes and the parsley. If desired the lamb may also be chopped in the processor, being careful not to overprocess.

## *Tomato Sauce*

See Basic Recipes, page 245.

# French Bread Toast

Slice thinly a loaf of French bread and spread each slice generously on both sides with unsalted butter. Sprinkle with salt and place the slices on a cookie sheet, then put into a 400-degree oven until lightly toasted.

# Salad with Feta Cheese

See Basic Recipes for romaine salad on page 241. Imported Greek feta cheese may be added to the oil and vinegar dressing or may be served on the side. If you serve the cheese, do not salt the dressing.

# Melon in Season

Slice and chill a ripe melon for several hours. Serve with a slice of lemon or lime.

# Elegant Dinners

# Menu 16
TO SERVE 6

Marinated Broccoli

Poulet Sauté aux Huitres
Capon with Oysters

Tomatoes Filled with Green Peas

Mousse au Chocolat

WINE
A Bordeaux such as Côtes de Blaye
or a California Grey Riesling.

## Shopping List

**Poultry**
4-lb capon cut into
  8 pieces

**Fish**
1 to 2 jars Olympia
  oysters

**Produce**
2 bunches broccoli
1 bunch celery
¼ lb mushrooms
6 tomatoes
2 lb fresh peas

**Groceries**
1 pt heavy cream
4-oz carton sour cream
4 oz semisweet
  chocolate

## Staples

sugar
olive oil
lemons (3)
garlic
parsley

butter (¾ lb)
onion
chicken stock
meat glaze

potato flour
eggs (6)
salt
pepper
vanilla extract

# Menu 16

This is an elegant menu, yet one especially easy to serve. The capon is extremely rich and does not call for potatoes, pasta or rice. A loaf of French bread, which has been warmed in the oven so that the crust is very crisp, is especially nice served with the broccoli. The chocolate mousse is one I learned from Chef Paul Quiaud of Ernie's Restaurant, and I have not found another to equal it.

## Planning Ahead

Make the broccoli well ahead of time and have it attractively arranged on individual plates when your guests sit down at the table. The capon, loosely covered, waits very nicely for several hours. When you are ready, reheat the sauce, add the oysters, and serve spooned over the re-warmed capon. The peas in tomato shells add lovely color to the plate.

# Marinated Broccoli

Wash and trim 2 bunches of broccoli. Cook according to the green vegetable method, page 242, until barely tender. When done, drain and carefully place in a flat serving dish and immediately, while still hot, pour over the following marinade: 8 tablespoons olive oil, 3 tablespoons freshly squeezed lemon juice, 1 peeled clove of garlic cut in half, 1 tablespoon freshly minced parsley, ½ teaspoon salt, ½ teaspoon pepper.

Allow to marinate 2 hours and serve at room temperature.

# Poulet Sauté aux Huitres
*Capon with Oysters*

Brown a 4-pound cut-up capon in 5 tablespoons unsalted butter, turning the pieces frequently. Then add 1 onion, 2 peeled stalks of celery, ¼ pound mushrooms, and 2 tablespoons parsley, all finely chopped. Cover the pot and continue cooking the chicken in a 350-degree oven for 25–30 minutes, or until done. Place the chicken pieces on a serving dish. Place the pot over the fire, add 1 cup chicken stock, and cook until it is reduced by one half. Add 1 tablespoon meat glaze (see page 240), 1 cup crème fraîche (see page 240) that has been mixed with 1 teaspoon potato flour, and allow to reduce again until the sauce is the consistency of heavy cream. Taste and correct the seasoning. Poach 1 to 2 cups Olympia oysters in their own liquid for 5 seconds, drain, and add to the sauce. This much can be prepared ahead. When ready to serve, reheat the sauce gently and spoon generously over the re-heated chicken. If Olympia oysters are not available, you may substitute large oysters, but be sure to cut them into 25-cent-sized pieces.

## Food Processor Method

You may chop the onions, celery, mushrooms and parsley in the processor, using the steel knife.

# Tomatoes Filled with Green Peas

Cut the tops off 6 firm, red tomatoes. Scoop out the centers carefully, sprinkle with salt, and turn upside down on towels to drain. Shell 2 pound fresh green peas and cook according to the green vegetable method (see page 242) until barely tender. Drain and return the peas to the saucepan and add ¼ pound unsalted butter. Place the tomatoes on a baking sheet and put into a 350-degree oven for 5 minutes. Remove from the oven and fill with the hot peas. Serve immediately or re-heat to serve.

# Mousse au Chocolat

In a double boiler over simmering, not boiling, water, melt 4 ounces semisweet chocolate, a pinch of salt, 4 tablespoons sugar, ½ teaspoon vanilla, and 2 ounces unsalted butter, stirring constantly. When well-blended, remove from the heat and stir in 4 egg yolks. Fold in very carefully—for this is the key to the lightness of the mousse—6 stiffly beaten egg whites and 1 cup whipped cream. Spoon into individual dishes and chill.

## Food Processor Method

The chocolate, sugar, vanilla, butter and egg yolks may be processed with the steel knife until well blended. The whisking of the egg whites and cream and the folding into the chocolate base must be done by hand.

# Menu 17

TO SERVE 8

## Coquilles Saint-Jacques
Scallops

## Roast Boned Leg of Lamb

## Torta de Melanzana
Eggplant Pie

## Watercress and Endive Salad

## Fresh Strawberry Soufflé

WINE
*With the scallops,
a white Bordeaux, Entre-Deux-Mers,
and with the lamb,
a red Bordeaux, a Graves,
or a California Gamay.*

# Shopping List

### Fish
½ lb tiny cooked
  shrimp
1 lb scallops

### Meat
5-lb leg of lamb, boned
  and left open

### Produce
½ lb mushrooms
6 shallots
1 medium-sized
  eggplant
4 ripe tomatoes
1 green pepper
2 bunches watercress
1 head of French
  endive
1 pt ripe strawberries

### Spirits
dry white wine
brandy

### Groceries
½ pt heavy cream
1 pt light cream
small bottle Japanese
  soy sauce
5 slices Mozarella
  cheese

# Staples

| | | |
|---|---|---|
| butter | parsley | salt |
| sugar | onion | pepper |
| lemon | white wine vinegar | powdered ginger |
| garlic | Dijon mustard | thyme |
| flour | eggs (12) | bouquet garni |
| vegetable oil | milk |   (see page 247) |

# Menu 17

This was the menu I chose to do for my first class. I wanted an impressive meal, and everyone was indeed impressed to see how easy it is to prepare an elegant meal in advance. The Coquille is a popular way to serve scallops; the lamb, roasted quickly and served rare, is succulent and tender; and the strawberry soufflè maintains a fresh strawberry taste. I am sure your guests will be as delighted with this dinner as my students were.

## Planning Ahead

Finish preparing the scallops and gently reheat them just before your guests arrive. Spoon them into shells and place the shells on a cookie sheet, ready to go into the oven. The scallops make a good hors d'oeuvre served about midway in the cocktail hour. Before the guests arrive, finish roasting the lamb and leave in a warm place, covered loosely with foil until ready to carve on the bias and serve. Allowing about an hour cooking time, pour the custard over the eggplant, and put it into the oven. As soon as the eggplant is finished, invite your guests to the table and then serve the meal. When the last guest has finished, remove the dinner plates, whisk the egg whites for the soufflé, then carefully fold them into the strawberry base. (The base may be made several hours ahead.) Put the soufflé into the oven, noting the time, and bring the salad with its dressing to the table. Toss and serve the salad, and by the time it is finished and the table is cleared, your soufflé will be ready. Have the plates, spoons, and forks for the soufflé, a trivet and a large serving spoon waiting on the table. Bring in the soufflé and enjoy the compliments.

# Coquilles Saint-Jacques
*Scallops*

Bring to a boil 1½ cups dry white wine with a bouquet garni (see page 247). Add 1 pound scallops, washed and drained, and a pinch of salt, and simmer for 1 minute. Drain the scallops, reserving the broth, and cut them into small, uniform pieces. Clean and chop ½ pound fresh mushrooms. Put them into a saucepan with 6 finely chopped shallots and 1 tablespoon finely chopped parsley. Add 2 tablespoons butter, 1 teaspoon lemon juice, and 2 tablespoons water. Cover and simmer for 10 minutes. Strain and add the liquor to the wine broth. Melt 4 tablespoons butter in a saucepan and add 4 tablespoons flour, stir with a wire whisk, add gradually the combined hot liquors, and cook, stirring constantly until the sauce is thickened and smooth. Add 3 or 4 tablespoons heavy cream. Correct the seasoning and stir in scallops, shallots, mushrooms, and ½ pound cooked tiny shrimp. Just before serving, reheat the scallop mixture, spoon into individual scallop shells, piling high in the center, and put into a preheated 450-degree oven for 5 minutes.

## Food Processor Method

Chop the mushrooms, shallots and parsley in the processor using the steel knife.

# Roast Boned Leg of Lamb

Have your butcher bone and leave flat a 5-pound leg of lamb. In a glass or enameled container marinate it in the following mixture. In a medium saucepan put ¾ cup dry white wine, ¾ cup Japanese soy sauce, 1 tablespoon freshly grated ginger, 1 tablespoon sugar, 2 crushed cloves of garlic, and ½ teaspoon crushed peppercorns. Bring to a boil and boil 1 minute. Cool and pour over the lamb. Marinate 2 or 3 hours. When ready to roast, pour off the marinade and put the lamb into a 450-degree preheated oven for 25 minutes for rare. Then put it under an extremely hot broiler or on the barbecue for 3 minutes each side to char. Let rest in a warm place at least 20 minutes before slicing and serving.

# Torta di Melanzana
## *Eggplant Pie*

Over a high flame fry slices of eggplant in hot oil until they are soft and delicately browned. Place a layer of eggplant slices in a large, flat pie dish or rectangular baking dish and season with salt, pepper, finely minced parsley, and dried thyme. Cover with a layer of sliced tomatoes. Sprinkle with salt, pepper, parsley, finely chopped onion, and chopped green pepper. Cover the tomatoes with thin slices of Mozzarella cheese. Beat 3 egg yolks into 1½ cups light cream and, 45 minutes before serving, pour over entire dish and bake uncovered in a 325-degree oven until done. To serve, cut like a pie.

### *Food Processor Method*

The eggplant, tomato and mozzarella cheese may be sliced in the processor using the 4 mm slicing disc. The green pepper, onion and parsley may be chopped in the processor using the steel knife.

# Watercress and Endive Salad

With mustard dressing. See Basic Recipes, page 241.

# Fresh Strawberry Soufflé

Prepare the soufflé dish (see page 245) and set aside. Melt 3 tablespoons butter in a saucepan, add 2 tablespoons flour, blend well, and cook until the mixture begins to boil. Add ½ cup warm milk and continue cooking, stirring constantly with a wire sauce whisk, for 3 or 4 minutes. Remove the pot from the fire and add 5 egg yolks that have been beaten lightly with 3 tablespoons sugar. Then add 1 cup finely chopped fresh ripe strawberries that have been mixed with 2 tablespoons of sugar and sprinkled with a little brandy. This much can be done several hours ahead. Thirty minutes before serving, whisk 6 egg whites until they are stiff and add 2 teaspoons sugar. Continue whisking for a moment. Pour the batter into the prepared soufflé dish and bake in a 400-degree oven for 20 to 25 minutes. Serve immediately.

## Food Processor Method

The strawberries may be chopped in the processor using the steel knife, the sugar and brandy added before chopping.

# Menu 18
## TO SERVE 8

Cream of Butter Lettuce Soup

Veal Kidneys in Madeira Wine Sauce

Pommes au Beurre

Lime Pie

WINE
A dry red Médoc or
California Cabernet Sauvignon.
With dessert, a Barsac or
Cream Sherry.

## Shopping List

**Meat**
4 veal kidneys, very
   light in color
16 tiny pork sausages

**Produce**
2 large heads of butter
   lettuce
24 mushrooms
6 limes

**Groceries**
½ pt whipping cream
1 can sweetened
   condensed milk
½ pt heavy cream

**Spirits**
Madeira wine

## Staples

chicken stock
butter
flour
milk

meat glaze
potato flour
beef stock (page 239)

parsley
eggs
salt
pepper

# Menu 18

This is a delicate, elegant meal, and my favorite way of preparing kidneys. The soup is an unusual and delicious way of serving a salad and the lime pie is refreshing. This is an easy menu to cook and serve. Lamb kidneys may be substituted for veal if desired.

## Planning Ahead

Prepare the soup well ahead and reheat to serve. The kidneys may also be finished before your guests arrive and reheated gently (being careful not to overcook the kidneys) just before serving. The pie needs at least 2 hours chilling time.

# Cream of Butter Lettuce Soup

Bring a cup of chicken stock to the boil, and add 2 large or 4 small washed heads of butter lettuce. Boil for 5 minutes. In a small saucepan melt 3 tablespoons butter, and 3 tablespoons flour, cook 2 minutes, and gradually stir in 1½ cups milk. Continue cooking until the béchamel thickens. If it is too thick, add a little chicken stock; if it is too thin, let it simmer a little longer. Add salt and pepper to taste. Lift out the lettuce and put it into the container of the blender, add the béchamel and a cup of whipping cream. Blend everything briefly. Return soup to a saucepan and gently reheat while you adjust flavor, seasoning, and thickness. Use as much chicken stock, tablespoon by tablespoon, as is needed to thin the soup to your personal taste.

*Food Processor Method*

The soup may be puréed in the processor using the steel knife.

# Veal Kidneys in Madeira Wine

Cut 4 veal kidneys in half and remove the fat and tubes. Then cut each half in about 3 pieces. Heat 3 tablespoons butter in a heavy skillet until it turns brown. Flour the kidney pieces lightly, spanking off any excess flour, and sauté them for 5 minutes on each side over medium heat. Remove them and add 24 mushrooms cut in quarters and cook over high heat for 1 minute. Remove mushrooms from pan. Meanwhile, in another skillet, sauté 16 tiny pork sausages cut in half for about 10 minutes until done. Drain on paper towels. Pour off the excess butter from the skillet in which you browned the kidneys and mushrooms. Add 1 tablespoon meat glaze (page 240) and 1 cup Madeira wine. Stir over a medium flame until it boils, scraping up all the brown bits left by the kidneys. Cook until the sauce thickens somewhat. Strain the sauce and taste for seasoning. Return the kidneys, mushrooms, and sausages to the pan, and add the sauce. Just before serving, heat through, being careful not to overcook the kidneys, and serve in a small casserole garnished with freshly minced parsley.

# Pommes au Beurre

Parboil 4 potatoes cut into small potato shapes (balls, ovals, etc.) for 5 minutes in salted water and drain them well. Sauté them to a rich golden brown in a generous amount of clarified butter (page 247). Season to taste with salt and pepper.

# Lime Pie

Prepare a tart pastry (page 244), chill and roll out to about ⅛ inch. Line an 8-inch tart tin with the pastry. Beat 3 egg yolks until thick, add 1 can sweetened condensed milk and ¾ cup freshly squeezed lime juice. Fold in 3 stiffly beaten egg whites and pour into the tart shell. Place the pie on the bottom of a 425-degree gas oven for 10 minutes or over the coils on top of an electric stove for 7 minutes, in order to brown the lower crust. Reduce oven heat to 350 degrees and finish baking on the rack for 10 to 15 minutes more. Serve chilled, garnished with whipped cream.

## Food Processor Method

Make the pastry in the processor using the steel knife—see page 7. In the bowl with the steel knife, process the egg yolks, add the milk and lime juice and process until well mixed. The egg whites cannot be whisked or folded in the processor.

# Menu 19

TO SERVE 8

*Fresh Salmon Soufflé*

*Marinated Roast Beef, Sauce Poivrade*

*Potatoes Boulangère*

*Watercress Salad*

*Chocolate Fudge Pie*

WINE
*A full-bodied red,*
*Saint-Emilion or Cent-Vignes*
*or a California Cabernet*
*Sauvignon.*

## Shopping List

*Fish*
1½ lb salmon filet

*Meat*
3- to 4-lb beef for
  roasting (filet,
  butterball, etc.)

*Produce*
1 bunch carrots
2 bunches watercress

*Spirits*
sherry wine
red wine

*Groceries*
1 pt heavy cream
2-oz package bitter
  chocolate
2 oz pistachio nuts

## Staples

butter
sugar
flour
milk
eggs
vegetable oil
onions
garlic
potatoes (5–6)

beef stock (2 cups),
  see page 239
parsley
chicken stock
tarragon vinegar
dry mustard
Dijon mustard
dried dill weed

thyme
bayleaf
cloves
black peppercorns
salt
pepper
cayenne pepper
bouquet garni
  (page 247)

# Menu 19

Don't be put off if at first glance this menu seems too rich. The fresh salmon soufflé is an exciting first course and the sauce for the beef is unusual. There was a highly critical student in one of my classes who was able to find something wrong with every dish I served. The fudge pie on this menu is so good I wondered what she would find to criticize about it. It amused me when, after finishing every crumb of the pie, her criticism was "a pinch too much salt in the pastry crust."

## Planning Ahead

The pie should be made in the morning and chilled. Be careful not to overbake it—it should be soft and fudgy. The salmon soufflé base can be prepared ahead and left to wait. The meat should be roasted and taken out of the oven to be kept warm, sauce already made, when the guests arrive. The potatoes should be cooked and kept in a warm place. After the last guest arrives put the soufflé into the oven. Be sure to note the time carefully, perhaps announcing, as I do, that there is a soufflé in the oven and everyone has to be seated in exactly 20 minutes. After that, my guests watch the time for me. When everyone is seated, bring the soufflé to the table and serve. Serve the beef, sliced thinly on the diagonal, with some sauce, and pass extra sauce for those who wish it. A salad of watercress with a mustard dressing is just right served next. The fudge pie is so rich, small slices will do.

# Fresh Salmon Soufflé

Grind twice, with the finest blade of your grinder, 1½ pounds salmon filet. In a small saucepan melt 3 teaspoons butter. Remove from the heat and add 2 teaspoons flour. Season to taste with salt, cayenne pepper, ½ teaspoon dry mustard, 1 teaspoon dried dill weed, and blend in ⅓ cup milk. Return the sauce to the flame and stir constantly with a wire sauce whisk until it boils. Remove from the heat and add 2 tablespoons sherry wine. Mix this sauce with the raw fish. This much can be prepared well ahead. Approximately 25 to 30 minutes before serving, fold in very carefully 1 cup stiffly whipped cream and 5 stiffly whisked egg whites. Spoon the mixture into a well-greased 2-quart soufflé dish and bake 25 minutes in a preheated 375-degree oven.

### Food Processor Method

The salmon may be ground in the processor using the steel knife. The seasoned béchamel sauce may be added to the salmon and processed until blended. The egg whites and cream cannot be whisked or folded in the food processor.

# Marinated Roast Beef

Select a 3- to 4-pound piece of your favorite cut of roasting beef—filet, butterball Châteaubriand, etc. Place the meat in the following marinade 2 hours before roasting. Combine 1 cup red wine, ½ cup tarragon vinegar, ½ teaspoon thyme, a bay leaf, 6 whole cloves, a sliced carrot and a sliced onion and 1 clove of minced garlic. When ready to roast, remove the meat from the marinade (reserving marinade) and put in to a 450-degree oven, allowing 8 minutes a pound for rare. Let stand in a warm place at least 20 minutes before carving thinly on the bias. Serve with Sauce Poivrade.

## Sauce Poivrade

Cook ½ cup chopped carrots, ½ cup chopped onions, and a bouquet garni (page 247) in butter until softened. Drain off the butter, add ¼ cup tarragon vinegar and ½ cup of the strained meat marinade to the vegetables, and cook over a high heat until it reduces to two-thirds of its original volume, stirring constantly. Add 1½ cups brown sauce (see following recipe) and simmer for 30 minutes. Add 8 crushed black peppercorns and simmer gently 10 minutes more. Correct the seasonings and strain. Just before serving bring the sauce to a boil, remove from the heat and swirl in 2 tablespoons butter.

### Food Processor Method

The carrots and onions may be chopped in the processor using the steel knife.

## Brown Sauce

In a saucepan melt 1½ tablespoons butter, add 1½ tablespoons flour, and stir with a wire sauce whisk until thoroughly blended and brown in color. Add gradually 2 cups strong beef stock (page 239), bring to a boil, then lower the heat and simmer for 20 minutes. Strain.

# Potatoes Boulangère

Peel and slice 5 or 6 potatoes. Peel and slice 1 small onion as thinly as possible. Mix the potatoes and onion together and season with salt, pepper, and 1 tablespoon freshly minced parsley. Put the mixture into a well-buttered ovenproof container and spread 4 tablespoons softened unsalted butter over the top. Add 4 ounces or more of chicken stock until the liquid comes halfway up the sides of the dish. Bake in a 400-degree oven for 30 to 40 minutes, until the potatoes are soft and the liquid is absorbed.

### Food Processor Method

The potatoes and onions may be sliced in the processor using the 4mm slicing disc.

# Watercress Salad

With mustard dressing. See Basic Recipes, page 241.

# Chocolate Fudge Pie

Prepare a tart pastry (see page 244), chill and roll out to about ⅛-inch thick. Line an 8-inch tart tin with the pastry. Cream ½ cup butter and add gradually 1 cup sugar. Add 1 teaspoon vanilla and blend thoroughly. Add 2 egg yolks, beating well after each addition. Add 2 ounces melted bitter chocolate, then add ½ cup sifted flour. Whisk 2 egg whites with a pinch of salt until they are stiff and fold into the chocolate mixture. Turn the filling into the pastry shell and place the pie on the bottom of a 425-degree gas oven for 10 minutes or over the coils on top of an electric stove for 7 minutes, in order to brown the lower crust. Reduce oven heat to 350 degrees and finish baking on the rack for 10 to 15 minutes more. Decorate with chopped pistachios and chill.

## Food Processor Method

Make the pastry in the processor, see page 7. Using the steel knife cream the butter and add the sugar and vanilla and process. With the machine running add the egg yolks, chocolate and flour—process until blended. The whisking and folding of the egg whites cannot be done in the processor.

# Menu 20

TO SERVE 6

Shrimp and Oyster Bisque

Sweetbreads in a Truffle Sauce

Tomatoes with Spinach Purée

Butter Lettuce and Parsley Salad

Fresh Raspberry Soufflé, Sauce Parisienne

WINE
*White Bordeaux: Graves,*
*White Burgundy: Pouilly-Fuissé, or a*
*California Pinot Chardonnay.*

# Shopping List

*Fish*
2 doz oysters in their
  shells *or*
2 8-oz jars shucked
  oysters

*Meat*
3 lb veal sweetbreads

*Produce*
1 stalk celery
3 shallots
6 tomatoes
2 lb spinach
2 heads butter lettuce
3 pt fresh raspberries

*Spirits*
white port wine
Madeira wine

*Groceries*
2 pts heavy cream
truffles, 1 or 2

## Staples

| | | |
|---|---|---|
| milk (5 cups) | vegetable oil | salt |
| parsley | tarragon wine vinegar | pepper |
| butter | sugar | cream of tartar |
| flour | lemon | vanilla beans or extract* |
| eggs (8) | mace | nutmeg |

*If vanilla extract is used, add after the custard has finished cooking.

# Menu 20

This is an elegant, rich dinner and one of the slightly more complicated to prepare. The sauce in which the sweetbreads are served is a combination of cream, white port, Madeira, and truffles, a heavenly blend of ingredients. The trick of the exceptional raspberry soufflé is that the flavor and texture of the fresh raspberries is held by sealing them with sugar syrup and giving them a minimum of cooking. For an appreciative audience, this menu is well worth the effort. Boned chicken breasts may be substituted for the sweetbreads; simply eliminate the blanching step.

## Planning Ahead

Blanch and skin the sweetbreads and press them between two plates the day or morning before dinner. The bisque may be prepared several hours ahead and reheated just before serving. Finish preparing the sweetbreads completely before the guests arrive, gently reheating just before serving. Have the spinach in the tomatoes ready to place in the oven when the bisque is served. Follow the method on page 245 for the soufflé.

# Shrimp and Oyster Bisque

Chop finely 2 cups each of shucked raw oysters and shelled raw shrimp. Reserve the oyster liquor. Put the oysters, shrimp, and oyster liquor in a heavy soup pot; add 4 cups milk, 1 cup heavy cream, ½ cup peeled minced celery, 3 tablespoons finely minced shallots, 1 tablespoon minced parsley, a pinch of mace, salt and pepper to taste. Simmer for 30 minutes. Put through a food mill or sieve. In a saucepan melt 3 tablespoons unsalted butter, stir in 3 tablespoons flour, and cook for 3 or 4 minutes. Stir into the bisque. One or 2 egg yolks may be added for increased richness.

### Food Processor Method

The oysters, shrimp, celery and shallots may be chopped in the processor using the steel knife.

# Sweetbreads in a Truffle Sauce

The preliminary preparation for sweetbreads is always the same. Soak the sweetbreads in cold water for an hour. Simmer them for 5 minutes in water to which the juice of a lemon has been added. Put them into ice water to stop their cooking and very carefully remove all of the membrane, fat, and tubing. Then press the sweetbreads between two plates with a weight on top to flatten them. Refrigerate for several hours.

Flour 3 pounds sweetbreads, spanking off the excess flour, and sauté them in foaming butter for 10 minutes on each side. Remove them from the heat and keep warm on a serving platter. Drain away the excess butter from the pan and add 1 cup heavy cream, 1 cup white port wine, and 1 cup Madeira wine. Add as many thinly sliced truffles with their juice as you can afford. Reduce the sauce to the consistency of heavy, thick cream. Season with salt and freshly ground white pepper. Gently warm the sweetbreads in the sauce, and serve.

# Tomatoes with Spinach Purée

Slice off the tops of 6 firm ripe tomatoes. Scoop out the pulp, sprinkle the shells with salt and pepper, and turn upside down to drain. Meanwhile make the spinach purée. Place the tomato shells on a greased baking sheet, put a dot of butter in each, and place in a 350-degree oven for 5 minutes. Remove, allow to cool slightly, and fill with hot spinach purée. Return to the oven for 5 minutes more and serve.

## *Spinach Purée*

Place 2 cups cooked, chopped spinach in the container of a blender. Add ½ to 1 cup béchamel sauce (see following recipe), spoon by spoon, and blend. Season to taste with salt, pepper, and freshly grated nutmeg.

### *Food Processor Method*

The spinach may be puréed in the processor instead of the blender using the steel knife.

## *Béchamel Sauce*

Melt 4 tablespoons unsalted butter, add 4 tablespoons flour, stir together, and cook for 5 minutes. Add 1½ cups or more of milk and cook until thickened.

# Butter Lettuce and Parsley Salad

With herb dressing. See Basic Recipes, page 241.

# Fresh Raspberry Soufflé

Measure 14 level tablespoons sugar into a heavy saucepan. Add 1 tablespoon water and bring to a solid boil, stirring continously with a wooden spoon to prevent the sugar from burning. Continue boiling until it reaches the "hard-ball" stage or until a candy thermometer reads between 250 and 255 degrees. This must be exact. Remove immediately from the heat and stir in 1 pound fresh raspberries. This much may be prepared ahead. Whisk 6 egg whites with ½ teaspoon cream of tartar. Quickly and carefully fold into the raspberries, pour into a prepared soufflé dish (page 245), and bake at 425 degrees for 15 to 20 minutes.

# Sauce Parisienne

Mix ½ cup vanilla sauce (see following recipe) with ½ cup puréed fresh raspberries. Fold in 1 cup whipped cream. Spoon over each serving of soufflé.

# Vanilla Sauce

Scald ½ cup each milk and heavy cream with a vanilla bean.* Beat 2 egg yolks with ¼ cup sugar and combine with the hot milk and cream, stirring with a whisk. Cook, stirring constantly, until the mixture thickens. Strain through a fine sieve and let cool.

*If vanilla extract is used, add after the custard has finished cooking.

# Menu 21
## TO SERVE 8

## Gravlax
Swedish Marinated Salmon

## Ground Meat Loaf in Pastry Crust

## Cucumber Salad

## Apricot Mousse

WINE
*A French medium Burgundy
such as a Pommard or
a California Pinot Noir.*

## Shopping List

**Fish**
2½ lb center-cut
  salmon filet

**Meat**
1 lb ground lean beef
1 lb ground lean pork
1 lb ground veal

**Produce**
¼ lb mushrooms
4 cucumbers

**Groceries**
1 pt sour cream
8 oz imported Swiss
  cheese
½ pt heavy cream
1 jar preserved
  lingonberries
thinly sliced white
  bread
1 lb dried apricots
4 oz slivered blanched
  almonds

## Staples

sugar
white cider vinegar
  (1½ cups)
lemons
Dijon mustard
vegetable oil

flour
butter
eggs
onions
parsley
milk
fresh dill

coarse salt
  (kosher salt)
peppercorns
dry mustard
salt
vanilla extract

# Menu 21

The first time this Scandinavian menu was prepared in class, a woman commented that she was Norwegian and one of the things she was happy to have left in Norway was the salted fish and pickled cucumbers. She continued that she had never eaten the fish and the cucumbers were always soggy. I didn't know quite how to respond and, embarrassed, continued preparing the meal. I was delighted when, after eating, she made a point of saying how much she regretted having not eaten gravlax all those years and how tasty and crisp she had found the cucumbers. Indeed, this is a delicious and lovely looking dinner.

## Planning Ahead

Again, everything should be prepared in advance. When the last guest arrives, I put the meat loaf into the oven, noting the time carefully. When it is taken out, transfer it immediately to a cutting board and let it stand in a warm place. The salmon, sliced and arranged in thin, overlapping slices on individual plates, can be on the table when the guests sit down. The mustard sauce is passed. The meat loaf, in its shiny crust, is a beautiful display to bring to the table. It must be sufficiently rested so that it does not fall apart when sliced—at least 20 minutes out of the oven. Sour cream and lingonberries, already on the table, may be passed. The cucumbers are served with the meat but on separate plates. The apricot mousse comes to the table any time you are ready.

# Gravlax
## Swedish Marinated Salmon

Have your fish dealer bone and cut in half lengthwise a 2½-pound center cut of fresh salmon. Place half the fish, skin side down, in a deep non-metal container. Wash and shake dry a bunch of fresh dill and place it on the fish. Combine ¼ cup coarse salt, ¼ cup sugar, and 2 tablespoons crushed peppercorns. Sprinkle this mixture evenly over the dill, then moisten with 1 teaspoon white vinegar. Top with the other half of the fish, skin side up; cover with foil and place a weight on top. Refrigerate 2 or 3 days, turning the fish every 12 hours, basting with the liquid marinade that accumulates. When the fish is finished, remove from the marinade, rinse away the seasonings, and pat it dry. Place the separated halves skin side down and slice the salmon halves thinly on the diagonal. Serve with toast or thin black bread, lemon wedges, freshly ground pepper, and mustard sauce.

## Mustard Sauce

In a blender container place 4 tablespoons Dijon mustard, 1 teaspoon dry mustard, 3 tablespoons chopped fresh dill, 3 tablespoon sugar, and 2 tablespoons white vinegar. Run blender a few seconds until mixture is a paste and then slowly pour in ⅓ cup vegetable oil until it forms a thick mayonnaise.

### Food Processor Method

With the steel knife in place, chop the dill. With the machine running, add the mustards, sugar and vinegar and process 2 or 3 seconds, then add the oil slowly.

# Ground Meat Loaf in Pastry Crust

Prepare the sour cream pastry on page 243, and chill. Sauté ¼ pound finely chopped mushrooms in 2 tablespoons foaming butter until soft. Set aside and in the same skillet sauté 1 pound ground lean beef, 1 pound ground lean pork and 1 pound ground veal. With a slotted spoon, draining the mixture of fat as you go, transfer the cooked meat and mushrooms to a large mixing bowl. Stir in ⅓ cup finely chopped onions, ¼ cup finely chopped parsley, 1 cup freshly grated imported Swiss cheese, and ½ cup milk. Combine and season with salt and pepper to taste. Cut the chilled pastry dough in half and roll out each half to a rectangle 6 by 14 inches, reserving any scraps. Butter a baking sheet; lift one sheet of the pastry over the rolling pin and onto the pan. Now place the meat mixture in the center of the dough. Pat the meat into a narrow loaf extending down the center of the dough. Gently drape the second sheet of pastry on top of the meat loaf and press the edges together with the tines of a fork. Roll out the scraps and cut into long narrow strips and decorate the top of the loaf. Brush the pastry with 1 egg beaten with 2 tablespoons milk and place in a preheated 375-degree oven for approximately 45 minutes or until the loaf has turned a golden brown. Serve thick slices of the hot loaf, accompanied by a bowl of sour cream and a side dish of lingonberries.

## Food Processor Method

The pastry may be prepared in the processor using the steel knife, see page 7. Again with the steel knife, chop the mushrooms, onions and parsley. Use the medium grating disc for the cheese. If desired, the meats may be chopped in the processor using the steel knife.

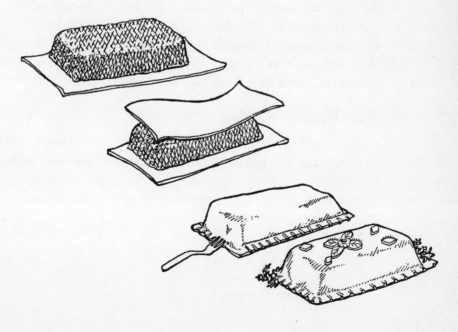

# Cucumber Salad

Score 4 large cucumbers, cut them in half lengthwise, and seed them with a teaspoon. Cut them into the thinnest possible slices and place in a single layer on paper towels. Sprinkle with salt, place more towels on top and a weight on top of the towels for an hour or so. Then remove the weight and gently pat the cucumbers dry with fresh towels. Place the slices in a shallow glass dish and pour over them the following marinade: Beat together 1¼ cups white vinegar, 2 tablespoons sugar, 1 teaspoon salt, and ½ teaspoon pepper. Chill and drain away the liquid before serving.

## Food Processor Method

Use the 2 mm slicing disc to slice the cucumbers.

# Apricot Mousse

Simmer 1 pound dried apricots in water to cover for 25 minutes. Stir in ½ cup sugar or more to taste and cook the fruit for 5 more minutes. Purée the apricots in a blender. Add ¼ pound melted unsalted butter. Stir in ¼ cup slivered toasted almonds. Whip 1 cup heavy cream and sweeten it to taste with sugar and vanilla. Fold the whipped cream into the puréed apricots and pour the mousse into small dessert dishes. Chill thoroughly.

## Food Processor Method

Purée the apricots with the steel knife, add the melted butter and process until blended. The cream cannot be whipped or folded in the processor.

# Menu 22
### TO SERVE 6

## Consommé Bruxelles
Consommé with Brussels Sprouts

## Turban of Sole Carmélite

## Pommes Nouvelles

## Butter Lettuce and Parsley Salad

## Frozen Lemon Cream

WINE
*A Meursault or a*
*California Sémillon*

## Shopping List

**Fish**
1¼ lb salmon filet
4 fillets of sole
½ pound raw shrimp

**Produce**
24 Brussels sprouts
¼ lb mushrooms
6 small artichokes
1 bunch watercress
24 small new potatoes
6 lemons for serving
  (optional)
lemons (3)

**Groceries**
1½ pt heavy cream
½ pt light cream
¼ lb Parmesan cheese
  (optional)

**Spirits**
dry white wine

## Staples

chicken or beef stock
  (7 cups)
butter
flour

eggs
parsley
sugar (1 cup)
milk

salt
white pepper

# Menu 22

The simple clear soup with Brussels sprouts is an understated beginning to this rich, elegant dinner. The ring of salmon and sole with artichoke hearts, mushrooms, and shrimp in a béchamel sauce is an intoxicating dish. The frozen lemon cream is refreshingly tart but sweet and rich at the same time. This is an often-requested meal by students and friends and a relatively easy and quick one to prepare.

## Planning Ahead

Finish preparing the soup, leaving the Brussels sprouts separate until ready to reheat and serve. The turban may be prepared hours ahead and placed in the refrigerator to wait for its final baking. The vegetables and shrimp can wait in the béchamel until time to reheat and serve. Thirty-five minutes before serving, put the turban into the oven. Let it rest 10 minutes before unmolding. The frozen lemon cream must be made well ahead and served frozen.

# Consommé Bruxelles
### Consommé with Brussels Sprouts

Wash 24 tiny Brussels sprouts and remove the outer leaves. Cook the sprouts according to special green vegetable method (page 242). Heat 6 cups home made stock (page 239) that has been clarified (see following). Add ¼ cup of the water in which the sprouts were cooked and correct the seasoning, adding salt and pepper as necessary. Put 4 sprouts in each soup plate and pour the hot consommé over them. If desired, grated Parmesan cheese may be passed with the soup.

147

### To Clarify Stock

Bring 7 cups strong homemade stock (page 239) to the boil, and add the lightly whisked whites from 3 eggs, the crushed shells may be added as well. Turn down the heat and allow to simmer approximately 10 minutes. Turn off the heat, let stand until cooled and strain through a very fine sieve.

# Turban of Sole Carmélite

Cut 4 thin filets of salmon from a filet weighing 1¼ pounds, and prepare a mousseline forcemeat (see following recipe) with the rest of the fish. Line a buttered ring mold with the 4 filets of salmon and 4 filets of sole that have been divided into 8 pieces. If possible, let the filets hang over the outside of the mold. Spoon the forcemeat gently into the mold and fold the ends of the filets over it. Press buttered wax paper over the mold and bake in a larger pan of hot water in a 400-degree oven for 20 minutes.

Cook ½ pound raw shrimp barely covered in half dry white wine and half water until they turn pink, about 30 seconds. Remove the shrimp, shell, devein, and set aside. Strain the liquid through a cloth and reserve. Sauté ¼ pound mushroom caps and 6 previously cooked small artichoke bottoms cut in half, in butter for 1 minute. In a heavy saucepan melt 3 tablespoons butter. Add 3 tablespoons flour, stirring constantly. Cook

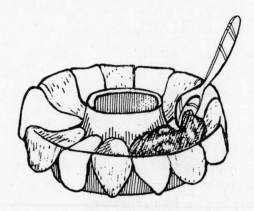

over a medium flame for 2 minutes and add ½ cup of the reserved shrimp liquid and about ¾ cup light cream stirring constantly. Cook until the sauce thickens to the consistency of very thick cream. Combine the shrimp, artichoke bottoms, and mushrooms and add to the sauce. Unmold the turban onto a heated platter and fill the center with the shrimp and vegetable mixture. Garnish with watercress.

## Mousseline Forcemeat

Run the remaining salmon filet, about ¾ pound, through the fine blade of a food chopper. Add ¼ teaspoon salt and a little white pepper. Gradually add the whites of 2 eggs, stirring vigorously with a wooden spoon. Place the bowl over cracked ice and gradually, using the wooden spoon, work in 1½ cups heavy cream. The mixture should be light and fluffy.

### Food Processor Method

With the steel knife process the salmon and seasonings approximately 40 seconds. With the machine running, gradually add the egg whites and process until mixture is smooth. Chill the mixture in the processor bowl for 1 hour. With the machine running, add the cream slowly, processing until it is absorbed into the fish.

# Pommes Nouvelles

Scrub the skins from 24 tiny new potatoes. Parboil in salted water for 3 minutes and dry them well. Heat 6 tablespoons butter in a heavy skillet, add the potatoes, salt and pepper, and cook until they are tender and golden brown all over. Sprinkle with finely chopped parsley just before serving.

# Butter Lettuce and Parsley Salad

See Basic Recipes, page 241.

# Frozen Lemon Cream

Stir 1 cup milk, 1 cup heavy cream, and 1 cup sugar over low heat until the sugar is thoroughly dissolved. Pour the mixture into a refrigerator tray and freeze it until it is mushy. Add the grated zest and juice of 3 lemons,* beat the mixture well with a rotary beater, and freeze it again for 2 hours. Beat the cream again thoroughly, return it to the freezer and freeze it until it is solid. The lemon cream may be served in scooped out lemon shells or long-stemmed sherbet glasses. Garnish with a lemon leaf.

*At this point the cream may be successfully made in an ice-cream freezer – following the manufacturer's suggested method.

## Food Processor Method

In the processor, using the steel knife, combine the milk, cream and sugar and process for 20 seconds. Leave the mixture in the processor bowl with the steel knife in the bowl and place in the freezer until mushy. Remove from the freezer, add the zest and juice and process for 1 minute. Return to the freezer for 2 hours, then process for 1 minute. Transfer to serving dishes or prepared lemon shells and freeze.

# Menu 23

TO SERVE 6

## Shrimp Sauté

## Caneton au Grand Marnier
Duckling in Grand Marnier Sauce

## Pommes de Terre à la Parisienne
Potatoes Parisienne

## Glazed Onions

## Plum Milk Sherbet

WINE
A French Vouvray or a
California Red Burgundy

# Shopping List

## Fish
1 lb raw shrimp

## Poultry
2 4-lb ducklings

## Produce
5 juice oranges
½ lb mushrooms
24 small white onions
1½ lb ripe plums
carrot ⎱
onion ⎰ for duck stock
celery

## Spirits
dry sherry wine
cognac
Grand Marnier

## Groceries
corn syrup

# Staples

butter
parsley
garlic
potato flour

potatoes
chicken stock
eggs
sugar

milk
lemons (4)
salt
pepper

# Menu 23

My objection to so many orange duckling recipes is that they are generally too sweet. I think you will find this is not the case with Caneton au Grand Marnier, a classic and very popular French dish. The plum milk sherbet is most unusual and a not-too-sweet end to this meal.

## Planning Ahead

Have the shrimp peeled and waiting next to the skillet with melted butter and parsley. Two minutes before serving, sauté quickly. The shrimp served in scallop shells make good hors d'oeuvre. The duck can be prepared ahead and left waiting in its sauce to be reheated. Do the same with the onions and potatoes. The plum sherbet is ready when you are, and is attractive served in long-stemmed glasses.

# Shrimp Sauté

Peel and devein 1 pound raw shrimp. Rinse and dry gently with a paper towel. In a large skillet heat 4 tablespoons unsalted butter and when it foams, add 3 tablespoons finely chopped parsley. Add the shrimp and sauté them for about 1 minute or until they are pink. Do not overcook them as they become tough and rubbery. Season with salt and pepper, and sprinkle with fresh lemon juice. Serve in scallop shells.

# Caneton au Grand Marnier
*Duckling in Grand Marnier Sauce*

Trim the wing tips and cut off the necks of 2 ducklings. Out of the wing tips, neck, and giblets, excluding the liver, make a duck stock (see page 239). Cut the ducklings into quarters, sprinkle with salt and pepper, and place them skin side up on a rack in a shallow roasting pan. Roast in a 400-degree oven, basting frequently with the fat that accumulates in the pan, about 35 minutes or until done. Remove the ducklings from the pan and set in a warm place. Add 1 tablespoon unsalted butter to ½ cup duck stock, fat removed, add the grated zest (page 57) of 1 orange, 1 cup sliced raw mushrooms, and 1 small clove of crushed garlic. Bring the mixture to a boil and simmer it gently for 2 minutes. Remove the pan from the heat and blend in 2 tablespoons potato flour mixed to a paste with 2 table-spoons duck stock. Stir in ¼ cup each dry sherry and cognac and ¾ cups each Grand Marnier and freshly squeezed orange juice. Return the pan to the heat and cook, stirring with a wire sauce whisk, until the mixture is smooth and thickened. Remove and discard the garlic and season to taste with salt and pepper. When ready to serve, heat the duck pieces in the sauce. Arrange the duck on a serving platter and spoon over the sauce. Garnish with thin slices of orange.

# Pommes de Terre à la Parisienne
*Potatoes Parisienne*

With a ball-cutter, scoop out potatoes in rounds smaller than hazelnuts. Sauté the potatoes in clarified butter (see page 247) until they are golden and soft. Sprinkle with chopped parsley and serve.

# Glazed Onions

Peel 24 small white onions and put them into a saucepan with 4 tablespoons melted butter. Add ¾ cup chicken stock, 1 tablespoon sugar, and ½ teaspoon salt, and let them cook very slowly, uncovered, over a low flame, until the onions are tender and the liquid is completely reduced.

# Plum Milk Sherbet

Beat 2 egg whites until they are stiff. Gradually beat in ¼ cup sugar, 2 cups milk, 1 cup corn syrup, and ⅔ cup lemon juice; transfer the mixture to a shallow dish and freeze. When the sherbet reaches the mushy stage, in about 2 hours, beat it again until it is smooth, then add 2 cups puréed cooked plums.* Return it to the freezer and, when it is almost solid, beat it again until smooth. Cover the dish and freeze the sherbet once more until it is firm.

*The sherbet may be successfully made in an ice-cream freezer.

# Menu 24
TO SERVE 8

### Carrot and Leek Bisque

### Roast Lamb, Sauce Béarnaise

### Pommes de Terre Dauphine
Deep-Fried Potato Puffs

### Butter Lettuce and Parsley Salad

### Gâteau au Chocolat et Marrons
Chocolate and Chestnut Cake

WINE
*A young Burgundy like Mâcon,
a Beaujolais, Moulin-à-Vent,
or a Cabernet Sauvignon or
Charbono from California.*

# Shopping List

**Meat**
6-lb leg of lamb *or*
4-lb boned leg,
   left open *or*
3 2-lb racks of lamb

**Produce**
6 carrots
4 leeks
2 shallots
2 heads butter lettuce

**Spirits**
dry white wine
dark rum

**Groceries**
1 pt heavy cream
4 oz sour cream
12 oz fresh chestnuts *or*
8 oz canned puréed
   chestnuts
6 oz semisweet
   chocolate

# Staples

chicken stock (5 cups)
parsley
eggs (12)
olive oil
tarragon vinegar

butter (¾ lb)
potatoes
vegetable oil
flour
sugar

powdered sugar
salt
pepper
chervil
whole peppercorns

# Menu 24

This is an elegant dinner to serve your gourmet friends. Both the carrot bisque and the chestnut cake are unusual and the béarnaise sauce a superb complement to the lamb. One of the students in my classes commented in amazement that the potatoes are so professional that they looked and tasted as good as in a restaurant!

## Planning Ahead

The cake may be finished several hours ahead and refrigerated. Finish preparing the soup and reheat it slowly before serving. Roast the meat and keep warm. The potatoes are best when served as soon as they are fried; however, if you wish, you may fry them in advance and place them on paper towels on a baking sheet in a barely warm oven—they keep nicely for an hour or so. The béarnaise reheats perfectly, as long as it is stirred constantly during reheating with a wire sauce whisk. When ready to serve the main course, arrange the lamb slices in the center of a serving dish, garnish with béarnaise, and surround with the potato puffs. Present at the table with extra béarnaise to pass. A butter lettuce and parsley salad is suggested.

# Carrot and Leek Bisque

Combine in a heavy soup pot 6 peeled carrots and 4 leeks, washed thoroughly and cut into 1-inch pieces. Add 5 cups chicken stock and salt and pepper to taste. Cook the vegetables covered about an hour or until they are very soft. In the container of the blender put ½ cup coarsely chopped parsley, add the vegetables and their broth and blend until the soup is thick and smooth. Just before serving, heat the soup, turn off the flame and add 3 egg yolks and 3 tablespoons crème fraîche (see page 240), stirring constantly. Reheat slowly, and serve garnished with minced parsley.

### Food Processor Method
Slice the carrots and leeks in the processor using the 6mm slicing disc. Using the steel knife, chop the parsley and add the cooked vegetables and broth and purée.

# Roast Lamb

For the roast lamb use a 6-pound leg of lamb or a 4-pound boned leg or three 2-pound racks of lamb. Preheat the oven for 30 minutes to 450 degrees, and have the lamb at room temperature. Rub the meat with a little olive oil, sprinkle with salt and pepper and place in the oven. For a 6-pound leg, 60 minutes is sufficient for rare; a 4-pound boned leg, left open and flat, 35 minutes for rare; a 2-pound rack, 25 minutes is adequate time for rare. For more well done, cook longer. When finished, remove the lamb from the roasting pan to the carving board, being careful not to pierce the meat, and let stand at least 20 minutes in a warm place before carving.

# Sauce Béarnaise

Combine 1 cup dry white wine, 2 tablespoons tarragon vinegar, 1 tablespoon finely chopped shallots, ¼ teaspoon chervil, and 2 peppercorns. Cook over a high flame until reduced to two-thirds of its original volume. Cool a little before adding 3 egg yolks slowly, stirring constantly over a very low flame, then add ½ pound unsalted butter, little by little, stirring until the sauce has the consistency of heavy cream. Serve over the lamb. Note: In order to insure a smooth sauce, use a wire sauce whisk to stir the béarnaise.

# Pommes de Terre Dauphine
*Deep-Fried Potato Puffs*

Make a mixture consisting of 2 cups of puréed potatoes and an equal amount of pâte à choux (see following recipe). Form little balls the size of a walnut, and drop into deep hot fat to puff and brown. Drain on paper towels, sprinkle with salt and pepper and serve hot.

## Pâte à Choux

Combine in a saucepan 1 cup water, 2 tablespoons butter, and ½ teaspoon salt. Bring the mixture to the boil and add 1 cup flour, all at once, stirring well until the mixture leaves the sides of the pan. Remove from the fire and add, one at a time, 4 whole eggs, beating well with a wooden spoon after each addition. This batter should be very soft but not liquid. If necessary another egg may be added.

### Food Processor Method

After the flour has been incorporated, transfer the dough to the processor. With the steel knife in place, add the eggs, one at a time, processing approximately 30 seconds, until the egg is absorbed before adding the next egg. The potatoes cannot be puréed in the processor.

# Butter Lettuce and Parsley Salad

With herb dressing. See Basic Recipes, page 241.

# Gâteau au Chocolat et Marrons
*Chocolate and Chestnut Cake*

Melt 3 ounces semisweet chocolate with 4 tablespoons water. Separate 4 large eggs, and beat the yolks with 8 tablespoons sugar until thick. Add the chocolate and 8 ounces puréed chestnuts (see following recipe). Whisk the 4 egg whites until stiff and fold into the chocolate mixture. Pour into two 8-inch greased and floured cake tins. Bake for 40 minutes at 350 degrees or until done (page 11). Handle this cake very delicately, letting it cool in the pan approximately 10 minutes before removing to a cake rack. After cooling, assemble cake, using chocolate cream described next.

### Food Processor Method

The yolks and sugar may be processed until thick in the processor bowl using the steel knife. With the machine running add the chocolate and chestnuts and process until smooth. The egg whites cannot be whisked or folded in the processor.

## Chocolate Cream

Melt 3 ounces semisweet chocolate in 3 tablespoons water. Beat in 2 egg yolks, 2 tablespoons powdered sugar, and 1 tablespoon dark rum. Cool. Whip 1 cup cream until thick and fold into the chocolate. it looks good if the mixture is left rather streaky. Sandwich the cakes together with the chocolate cream, reserving some to spread over the top of the cake. Refrigerate until ready to serve.

### Food Processor Method

Process the egg yolks, sugar and rum in the processor bowl using the steel knife. Add the melted chocolate and process until smooth. The cream cannot be whipped or folded in the processor.

## Puréed Chestnuts

With a sharp knife, cut a slit on the convex sides of the shells of the chestnuts. Bake them on an oiled baking pan at 450 degrees for 5 or 6 minutes. When the chestnuts are cool enough to handle, remove the shells with a sharp knife. Simmer them in milk until soft and then purée. Canned puréed chestnuts may be used when the fresh are not available.

### Food Processor Method

Using the steel knife, you may purée the chestnuts in the processor.

# Menu 25

TO SERVE 6

## Cheese Soufflé

## Poisson Braisé à la Dieppoise
Fish Braised Dieppe Style

## Carottes Vichy

## Pommes Rissolées

## Tarte aux Pommes à la M. Lecourt
M. Lecourt's Apple Tart

WINE
*California Pinot Blanc or Folle Blanche,*
*Chilean Riesling or*
*German Bernkasteler*

## Shopping List

### Fish
3½-lb whole white fish
  *or* 3 lb white fish
  filets
enough mussels to make
  a cup shelled *or*
8 oz Olympia oysters
6 oz tiny cooked
  shrimp

### Produce
3 shallots
2 doz tiny carrots
4 tart green apples
18 small red potatoes

### Spirits
dry white wine
Calvados (apple
  brandy)

### Groceries
8 oz imported Swiss *or*
  Gruyère cheese
½ pt heavy cream
4 oz sour cream

## Staples

butter
flour
milk

Dijon mustard
eggs
parsley

sugar
salt
cayenne pepper

# Menu 25

This menu and the two following were created after a delightful time I spent in Dieppe on the French coast of Normandy. While I was there I attended classes in Norman cooking offered by the charming M. Lecourt, former chef-owner of a well-known restaurant near Rouen. The cheese soufflé and fish are from his classes. He was kind enough to share with me his unusual apple tart recipe, which is his own invention, as is the method for browning pastry crusts used throughout this book. Here is a delicious and typically Norman menu.

## Planning Ahead

Every dish may be prepared in advance. For the cheese soufflé, follow the method for salmon soufflé, page 129. The fish may be finished, and reheated with the sauce just before serving. Finish cooking and reheat the carrots and potatoes. Be certain not to overcook the custard on M. Lecourt's tart. An impressive method of serving the main dish is to place the fish in the middle of a large serving tray. Surround it with the carrots and potatoes, garnish with minced parsley, and bring it to the table.

# Cheese Soufflé

In a heavy saucepan, melt 2 tablespoons butter, stir in 2 tablespoons flour, and cook 2 minutes over a medium flame. Add ¾ cup warmed milk. Turn to a low flame and cook an additional 5 minutes until the sauce thickens. Season with salt and cayenne pepper and 1 teaspoon Dijon mustard. Remove from the heat and add 3 egg yolks alternately with a generous cup of shredded imported Swiss or Gruyère cheese. Return to the stove,

165

melting the cheese over a low heat and stirring constantly. This much may be done well ahead. Twenty minutes before serving, fold in 5 stiffly beaten egg whites and pour into a generously buttered soufflé dish. Bake in a 400-degree oven 20 minutes. Serve immediately.

## Food Processor Method

Using the medium shredding disc, grate the cheese in the processor.

# Poisson Braisé à la Dieppoise
## Fish Braised Dieppe Style

Butter generously a flat ovenproof dish. Sprinkle with 3 tablespoons finely chopped shallots. Place a 3½-pound firm-fleshed white fish or 3 pounds of firm fish filets on top of the shallots; season with salt and cayenne pepper and pour enough dry white wine over the fish to barely cover. Press a buttered wax paper over the fish and place in a 375-degree oven for approximately 20 minutes. If using a whole fish, turn after 10 minutes. Be careful not to overcook. When the fish is done, remove from the pan and keep it warm.* If a whole fish is used, remove the bones and skin at this point. Reduce the braising liquid left in the pan by half, using a medium heat, and add 6 or more generous tablespoons crème fraîche (see page 240). Allow the sauce to boil down to the consistency of thick heavy cream. Add a cup of raw mussels or Olympia oysters and a cup of tiny cooked shrimp. When ready to serve, reheat the sauce gently and spoon over the fish. Garnish with a little chopped parsley.

*See pages 8 and 9 for reheating and keeping warm.

## Food Processor Method

Chop the shallots in the processor, using the steel knife.

# Carottes Vichy

Cook 2 dozen tiny peeled whole carrots uncovered in boiling Vichy water to which a teaspoon of sugar and a tablespoon of butter have been added. When the carrots are tender, drain if any liquid remains. Add a generous amount of butter, season with salt and white pepper, and sprinkle with finely chopped parsley. If baby carrots are not available, buy the smallest carrots and trim them to the size of baby carrots.

# Pommes Rissolées

Scrub and place in a saucepan 18 tiny red potatoes. Add water to cover, a little salt, and bring to a boil. Boil for 3 minutes. Drain, melt 4 tablespoons butter in an ovenproof dish, add the potatoes, and roast in a 350-degree oven until tender. Sprinkle with salt and pepper. If small red potatoes are not available, cut larger potatoes into balls.

# Tarte aux Pommes à la M. Lecourt
*M. Lecourt's Apple Tart*

Roll out a tart pastry (page 244) and line a well-buttered 8-inch tart pan or flan ring. Peel 3 Pippin or other tart green apples and slice in ¼-inch-thick slices. Arrange in overlapping circles, one layer deep, over pastry on the

bottom of the pan. Beat 2 eggs, add 2 heaped tablespoons sugar and 5 heaped tablespoons crème fraîche (see page 240). Mix well and add 2 tablespoons Calvados. Pour the custard over the apples. Preheat the oven to 425 degrees and put the tart on the floor of a gas oven for 10 minutes or over the coils on top of an electric stove for 7 minutes, in order to brown the bottom crust. Then lower the oven to 350 degrees and place the tart on the oven rack for an additional 10 or 15 minutes until the pastry is browned and the custard set.

## Food Processor Method

Make the pastry in the machine, see page 244. Slice the apples using the 4 mm slicing disk.

# Menu 26

TO SERVE 8

## Soupe de Poisson
Fish Soup

## Côtes de Porc Farcie de M. Jean Tilquin
M. Jean Tilquin's Stuffed Pork Chops

## Potatoes Clemenceau

## Butter Lettuce and Parsley Salad

## Tarte Normande

WINE
From Bordeaux, a Pomerol, or
a good Grignolino from California

## Shopping List

*Fish*
3 lb white fish, skin
   and bones

*Meat*
8 1¼-inch-thick
   center-cut pork chops
8 thin slices boiled ham

*Produce*
4 leeks
4 tomatoes
½ lb mushrooms
8 tart green apples
1 lb fresh green peas

*Spirits*
dry white wine

*Groceries*
8 thin slices imported
   Gruyère cheese
thin-sliced white bread
apricot jam

## Staples

butter (1 lb)
vegetable oil
garlic
sugar
chicken or veal stock
potatoes (2 lb)

flour
eggs
powdered sugar
thyme
bay leaf

saffron
salt
black pepper
white pepper
sage

# Menu 26

Even though Norman cooking is a provincial style of cookery, it is extraordinarily subtle and delicate. The clear fish soup in this menu is so subtly seasoned that I was unable to identify the saffron when I first tasted it. The stuffed pork chop is an invention of M. Jean Tilquin, chef-owner of the Hotel d'Univers in Dieppe. It is the most delicious way I know of preparing pork chops. Another apple tart, typically Norman, is a part of this menu.

## Planning Ahead

The tart should be prepared in advance and allowed to cool to room temperature. The soup can be finished and reheated before serving. The pork chops keep nicely for several hours and need only be reheated in their sauce just before dinner. The potatoes, mushrooms and peas may also be prepared ahead and reheated. My favorite way of serving the main course is to place the pork chops down the center of a large serving platter surrounded by the potatoes and vegetables. Sprinkle the chops with minced parsley, bring the platter to the table, and serve.

# Soupe de Poisson
*Fish Soup*

Clean well and cut into cubes the white parts of 4 leeks. Sauté over a low flame for 5 minutes in 1 tablespoon butter and 1 tablespoon vegetable oil. Add 2 cloves of garlic cut in half, a teaspoon or more of dried thyme, a bay leaf, and 4 medium tomatoes, cut in quarters. Add 3 pounds of white fish, skin, bones and all, cut into pieces, and cover with cold water. Add

¼ teaspoon saffron and ½ teaspoon sugar. Bring to a boil, cover and simmer 40 minutes. Pour the soup through a fine sieve, pressing down hard on the fish and vegetables to extract all the flavors. Strain once again to make certain the broth is perfectly clear. Return the soup to the pot, taste for seasonings, and add salt, white pepper, and more saffron if desired. Simmer uncovered until the broth is cooked down to a rich flavor. Serve with freshly made croutons.

### Food Processor Method

The leeks, garlic and tomatoes may be coarsely chopped in the processor using the steel knife. The soup cannot be "sieved" in the processor.

## Croutons

Cut off the crusts from 4 thinly sliced pieces of white bread. Cut into small dice and sauté in hot butter until golden brown. Remove with a slotted spoon and drain on paper towels.

# Côtes de Pork Farcie de M. Jean Tilquin
### *M. Jean Tilquin's Stuffed Pork Chops*

Slit eight 1¼-inch-thick center-cut pork chops to the bone. Sprinkle the opened chop with salt and pepper, spread generously with fresh or dried sage; place a thin slice of boiled ham and a slice of imported Gruyère cheese in the opening and close the chop. Season the outside lightly with salt and pepper. Melt 3 tablespoons butter in a large heavy skillet and sauté the chops, covered, over low heat, 10 minutes for each side. Remove to a serving dish and keep warm.* Pour out any excess fat remaining in the pan and add ½ cup dry white wine and ½ cup chicken or veal stock. Reduce rapidly over a high flame, taste for seasoning, and when ready to serve, spoon the sauce over each chop. Note: Do not overstuff the chops or the cheese will run out while cooking.

*See pages 8 and 9 for reheating and keeping warm.

# Potatoes Clemenceau

Peel and cut 2 pounds potatoes into small uniform dice and fry them in clarified butter (see page 247) until tender. Combine the potatoes with a scant ½ pound thinly sliced mushrooms that have been sautéed in butter for 1 minute. Add 1 cup fresh green peas, barely cooked until tender (the green vegetable method, page 242) and drained. Season with salt and pepper to taste.

# Butter Lettuce and Parsley Salad

See Basic Recipes, page 241.

# Tarte Normande

Roll out a tart pastry (page 244) and line a well-buttered 8-inch tart pan or flan ring. Peel 4 tart apples, cut into quarters, and put them into a heavy saucepan with a tablespoon of water and 3 tablespoons finely granulated sugar. Cook until soft, press through a sieve, and cool. Cover the bottom of the tart pastry with the apple sauce, about ½ inch thick, and then cover with thin slices of apple, arranged in overlapping circles. Preheat the oven to 425 degrees and put the tart on the bottom of a gas oven for 10 minutes or over the coils on top of an electric stove for 7 minutes, in order to brown the lower crust. Then lower the oven to 350 degrees and place the tart on the oven rack for an additional 10 or 15 minutes until the pastry is browned. Glaze with apricot jam diluted with a little water and boiled until thick, or cover immediately after baking with powdered sugar.

## Food Processor Method

The pastry may be made in the processor( page 244), the cooked apple puréed with the steel knife, and the raw apples sliced using the 4 mm slicing disc.

# Menu 27

Scallops au Naturel

Poulet Vallée d'Auge
Chicken Normandy Style

Green Beans with Parsley

Cottage-Fried Potatoes

Butter Lettuce and Parsley Salad

Benedictine Soufflé

WINE
A Vouvray or a
California Emerald Riesling

# Shopping List

*Fish*
1½ lb scallops

*Poultry*
2 2-lb chickens

*Produce*
1 lb mushrooms
2 lb fresh green
  beans
3 shallots
2 heads butter lettuce

*Spirits*
Calvados
Benedictine

*Groceries*
¼ pt sour cream
½ pt heavy cream

# Staples

| | | |
|---|---|---|
| butter | milk | tarragon vinegar |
| parsley | potatoes (6) | salt |
| chicken stock | sugar | pepper |
| lemons | chicken fat (¼ cup) | bay leaf |
| eggs (7) | vegetable oil | thyme |
| flour | | |

# Menu 27

Dieppe's fishing fleet supplies over half the scallops to France; consequently scallops are served frequently in Dieppe. The scallops offered on this menu are prepared in the very simplest and, I think, most elegant manner. The chicken is typically Norman, using both Calvados and cream. The soufflé is made from Benedictine, a liquor distilled in Normandy.

## Planning Ahead

The chicken and sauce may be prepared ahead and held separately, the sauce to be reheated slowly and spooned over the chicken just before serving. Both the green beans and the potatoes also reheat nicely. Have the scallops washed and waiting next to a heavy skillet with melted butter. Should you decide to serve them as an hors d'oeuvre, midway into the cocktail hour, flour and sauté the scallops quickly. Spoon into waiting scallop shells, sprinkle with parsley, put a small wedge of lemon on the side and serve immediately. For the soufflé, follow the method on page 245.

# Scallops au Naturel

Wash 1½ pounds scallops, removing any bits of shell or black threads. Dry them well, season with salt and pepper, and roll lightly in flour. Melt 5 tablespoons butter in a heavy skillet and sauté the scallops over a medium flame 1 minute each side. They should be a nice golden color. Do not overcook or they will become tough. Serve in scallop shells. If necessary, melt more butter to pour over the scallops. Garnish with chopped parsley and thinly sliced lemons.

# Poulet Valée d'Auge
*Chicken Normandy Style*

Cut two 2-pound chickens into 6 pieces each. (Reserve the innards, wing tips, and backs for the stock pot.) Season with salt and pepper and sauté in a heavy deep skillet in plenty of hot butter until golden brown on both sides. Remove the chicken and add 1 pound finely sliced mushrooms and 3 finely minced shallots. Cook about a minute, tossing frequently, and return the chicken to the pot. Flame the chicken with ½ cup or more Calvados. After the flame dies, add a bay leaf and a teaspoon each of thyme and parsley. Cover the pot and cook approximately 10 minutes more or until done. Take the chicken out, put into a serving dish and keep warm.* Add 8 tablespoons of crème fraîche (see page 240) to the juices remaining and cook the sauce down to the consistency of heavy cream. Season with salt and pepper to taste. Spoon the sauce over the chicken and serve.

*See pages 8 and 9 for reheating and keeping warm.

## Food Processor Method
Slice the mushrooms in the processor, using the 2 mm disc, and mince the shallots with the steel knife.

# Green Beans with Parsley

Cut 2 pounds fresh green beans into 1-inch lengths and cook them in chicken stock, using the green vegetable method (see page 242), until just barely tender. Drain, and toss the beans with ⅓ cup each of melted butter and minced parsley and 2 tablespoons fresh lemon juice. Salt and pepper to taste.

# Cottage-Fried Potatoes

Slice 6 hot, freshly boiled potatoes and brown them quickly in chicken fat or bacon drippings. Season with salt and pepper.

*Food Processor Method*

Allow to cool and slice using the 6 mm slicing disc.

# Butter Lettuce and Parsley Salad

See Basic Recipes, page 241.

# Benedictine Soufflé

In a medium-sized heavy saucepan, melt 3 tablespoons butter. Remove the pan from the fire, add 2 tablespoons flour, blend well, and return the pan to the heat. Continue cooking the butter-flour mixture until it bubbles slightly. Remove from the heat and blend in ¾ cup hot milk, Place the pan over the flame and stir until the sauce becomes very thick and boils. Stir it for 5 minutes, from the beginning of the boiling. Then remove from the heat and rapidly stir in 5 egg yolks that have been beaten with 3 tablespoons sugar. Add 6 tablespoons Benedictine. Whisk 6 egg whites until they are stiff but not dry, add 2 teaspoons sugar, and continue beating for another 30 seconds. Carefully fold the whites into the base and fill a prepared soufflé dish (page 245) with the mixture. Bake in a 400-degree oven for 20 to 25 minutes. Remove from the oven, take off the paper collar, and serve immediately.

# A Holiday Dinner

# Menu 28

## TO SERVE 8 TO 12

Oyster Stew

Roasted Turkey

Tarragon Crumb Stuffing

Sausage Stuffing

Madeira Cream Sauce

Puréed Turnips and Potatoes

Cranberry Apples

Romaine Lettuce Salad

Nancy Griffiths' Dinner Rolls

Pumpkin Custard Pie

WINE
California Green Hungarian
or Ohio Catawba.

# Shopping List

### Fish
3 doz oysters

### Meat
2½ lb ground pork
12- to 15-lb (fresh)
  turkey

### Produce
1 lb shallots
1 bunch parsley
8 turnips
6 baking potatoes
3 heads romaine lettuce
1 small pumpkin
  (or canned)

### Spirits
cognac
dry white wine
Madeira wine

### Groceries
2 qt whipping cream
1 cup cranberry juice
1 lb can of pumpkin *or*
  fresh pumpkin
1 package dry yeast
1 large loaf French *or*
  Italian bread

## Staples

butter (2½ lb)
chicken stock
  (page 239)
garlic
vegetable oil
red wine vinegar
eggs (9)
sugar

milk (3 cups)
unbleached white flour
  (6 cups)
stock concentrate
  (1 cup)
salt, pepper,
cayenne pepper,
tabasco

tarragon, thyme,
sage, mace, paprika
cinnamon, cloves,
nutmeg
cheesecloth
cooking foil
kitchen twine
  (to truss turkey)

# Menu 28

For the past couple of years, my Thanksgiving dinners have included 25 to 30 people. For such a large group, a buffet had to be created. This same menu, with your own variations appropriate to the occasion and the season, could be used for any festive gathering or holiday meal. Every recipe doubles or triples beautifully to accommodate a larger group.

## Planning Ahead

The day before, make the yeast dough and refrigerate. Prepare the two stuffings and refrigerate. Prepare and refrigerate the pastry for the pies. Make the pumpkin custard filling and the cranberry apples·and refrigerate. First thing the next morning, stuff the turkey with both fillings and put it into the oven. Next, roll out the pastry crusts and finish the pies. Prepare the turnips and potatoes and leave in the pot for reheating. Take the chilled ·yeast dough from the refrigerator, roll it out, and cut it into rolls. Let rise and, when they have doubled in bulk, bake them. When the turkey is done, take it out of the oven and let it stand at least 1 hour before carving. When ready to carve, remove the stuffings and place them in attractive containers ready to reheat. Carve the turkey, arranging it on platters of all white meat and all dark meat. Covered with foil, the turkey stays succulent at room temperature until ready to serve. Prepare and chill the salad greens, make the salad dressing and the Madeira cream sauce for the turkey.

Since holidays are a family affair and include children, I invite my guests to come at five in the afternoon. Just before they arrive, everything is reheated except the turkey, which I prefer at room temperature. For a buffet, I arrange things on the table, with hot dishes on electric food warmers. At six o'clock everyone is invited to eat. Since each person helps himself, I am able to relax and enjoy the evening. For a large party, the oyster stew is eliminated only because service is difficult. For a small dinner, it is a wonderful addition to the menu.

# Oyster Stew

Poach 3 dozen shucked oysters in their own liquor over a low flame for 1 minute. Scald 6 cups half cream and half milk. Just before serving, reheat the cream and combine the oysters, their liquor, 3 tablespoons butter, salt, pepper and cayenne to taste. Serve as the butter is melting.

# Tarragon Crumb Stuffing

Make approximately 10 cups fresh white French or Italian bread crumbs in the blender or food processor. Place 2 cups finely chopped shallots and 1 pound butter in a saucepan to melt. Add the bread crumbs, 2 tablespoons or more of chopped dried tarragon, ½ cup minced parsley, 1 teaspoon salt and pepper, or to taste, and mix well. Add enough chicken stock, starting with 2 ounces, so that the stuffing holds together nicely. Stuff the larger cavity of the turkey, place a piece of folded foil in the opening, and secure.

## Food Processor Method

Using the steel knife, process the bread crumbs in several batches, then the shallots, the tarragon and parsley.

# Sausage Stuffing

Combine the following ingredients: 2½ pounds ground pork, 1 finely chopped clove of garlic, ¼ cup finely chopped parsley, 2 teaspoons salt, ¼ teaspoon freshly grated nutmeg, 1 teaspoon freshly ground black pepper, ¼ teaspoon cayenne pepper, 1 teaspoon thyme, 1 teaspoon ground sage, and 1 tablespoon cognac. Blend well, fill the neck cavity of the bird and secure. You will have too much sausage stuffing, so place the surplus in a covered casserole and bake it separately.

### Food Processor Method

Using the steel knife, chop the garlic, add the parsley and chop, then add the meat and process until desired texture is achieved. (When chopping the meat, check after each pulse for the texture.)

# Roasted Turkey

For a 12- to 15-pound bird: After you have stuffed the bird, truss it securely, rub the turkey's skin well with butter, and sprinkle with salt, pepper and paprika. Place the bird on its side in a roasting dish and cover with a piece of cheesecloth. Roast the turkey at 375 for an hour. Baste and turn on its other side for an hour more, baste again and turn the bird on its back, breast side up, and roast approximately 1 hour and 20 minutes more. Allow about 15 minutes a pound all together. Baste often, at each turn-and-baste step, the cheesecloth should be replaced over the top of the turkey. If there are not enough pan juices for basting, add butter and white wine. Turkey is done when legs and thighs move up and down freely. For a more accurate test, a meat thermometer inserted into the deepest part of the breast should read about 170° F. Allow the turkey to stand at least 1 hour before carving.

# Madeira Cream Sauce

Pour off the fat from the roasting pan and add 1 cup Madeira wine, ¼ cup water, ¼ cup cognac, and 1 cup stock concentrate (page 240). Bring to a boil, scraping up all the browned coagulated juices sticking to the bottom of the roasting pan. Reduce the sauce to 1 cup and strain into a saucepan. Add 1½ cups whipping cream and reduce to the right consistency (page 6). Taste and season with salt and freshly ground white pepper. Reheat when ready to serve.

# Carving A Turkey

Remove the stuffing from both cavities of the bird and transfer to serving bowls. Cover and keep warm until ready to serve or let stand in a cool place and reheat to serve.

Place the turkey on a large cutting board with a well. Using a small straight carving knife and a two tined fork, cut the skin all around the thigh. (1) Gently pull off the leg and thigh, using your knife to hold the bird steady. Separate the thigh from the drumstick at the joint. (2, 3) Slice the thigh and the drumstick, arranging the dark meat on the platter. (4, 5) Cut the breast into thin slices and arrange on the same platter. Separate the wing at the joint, adding the wing to the white meat on the platter. Repeat the same procedure for the other side. Carving method would be the same for any poultry.

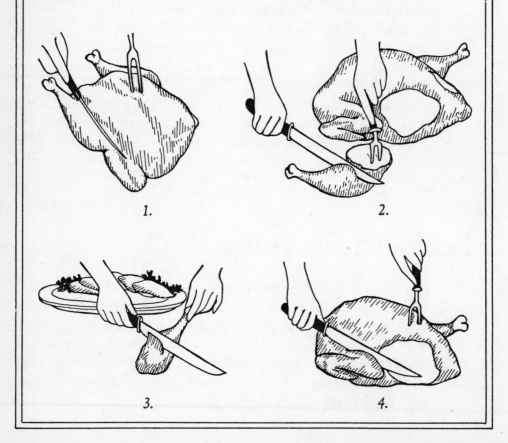

1.                    2.

3.                    4.

# Puréed Turnips and Potatoes

Peel and slice 8 turnips and 6 baking potatoes. Cook separately in boiling salted water until tender. Drain and purée through the fine disc of a food mill. Combine the puréed turnips and potatoes and work in ½ pound or more of unsalted butter. Season well with salt and freshly ground white pepper. Reheat when ready to serve.

## Food Processor Method

The turnips may be sliced in the processor, using the 4mm disc. After cooking, use the steel knife to purée in batches, with the butter and seasonings. The potatoes cannot be puréed in the processor.

# Cranberry Apples

Boil together, for 3 minutes, 1 cup each of cranberry juice and sugar. Peel and dice 4 tart apples. Drop the apples a few at a time into the boiling syrup and cook them for about 6 minutes, or until just tender. Remove the fruit from the syrup and serve as a garnish with the turkey.

# Romaine Lettuce Salad

With oil and vinegar dressing. See Basic Recipes, page 241.

# Nancy Griffiths' Dinner Rolls

Mix 1 package dry yeast with 1 tablespoon warm water and 3 teaspoons sugar. Let stand 5 minutes. Scald and cool 1 cup milk. Cream together ½ cup butter and ¼ cup sugar, add 3 well-beaten eggs and the yeast mixture.

Add 4 cups white flour alternately with the scalded milk. Let the dough stand in the mixing bowl in a warm place to rise. After 2 to 3 hours, punch it down, cover, and refrigerate overnight. Roll out and cut into round shapes, place on an ungreased cookie sheet, and let rise again. Bake in a 400-degree oven for 8 minutes. Makes approximately 3 dozen rolls.

### Food Processor Method

The bread dough may be mixed in the processor, using the steel knife.

# Pumpkin Custard Pie

Make enough tart/pie pastry (page 244) for 2 pies. Allow dough to rest in the refrigerator at least 1 hour. Roll out to ⅛ inch thickness, and line two 9-inch pie or tart molds. Place 2 cups puréed cooked pumpkin in a bowl. Add 6 lightly beaten eggs combined with 2 cups heavy cream, ¼ teaspoon salt, ¼ teaspoon pepper, ¾ cup sugar, 1 teaspoon ground cinnamon, ¼ teaspoon ground cloves, ½ cup cognac, and ¼ teaspoon ground mace. Blend thoroughly. Correct the seasoning—you may want a spicier pie. Fill the pie shells and place the pies on the bottom of a 425-degree gas oven for 10 minutes of over the coils on top of an electric stove for 7 minutes, in order to brown the lower crust. Finish baking on the rack of a 350-degree oven about 10 minutes more until the custard is just set. Serve at room temperature with cognac-flavored and sweetened whipped cream.

### Food Processor Method

Make the pastry in the processor, (page 244). If you are using fresh pumpkin, it may be cooked and then puréed in the processor, using the steel knife. The eggs, cream, salt, sugar and seasonings may be added and blended in the processor.

# Large Buffet Dinners

# Menu 29

TO SERVE 10

Broiled Herbed Chicken Legs

Sliced Roast Veal with Mustard Sauce

Sausage Baked in Pastry

Steak Tartare

Marinated Mushrooms

Cucumbers in Sour Cream

Guacamole Salad

Assorted Breads and Toast

Strawberry Bavarois

WINE
*Anything goes,
a selection of your favorite
red and white table wines
and beers.*

## Shopping List

**Meat**
10 chicken legs
3-lb veal rib roast
1½-lb whole French or
   Italian sausage
1 lb beef, round,
   sirloin or tenderloin

**Produce**
1 bunch chives
1 lb mushrooms
3 large cucumbers
3 ripe avocados
1 large tomato
1 sweet green pepper
4 cups ripe strawberries

**Spirits**
cognac

**Groceries**
small jar sour pickles
small jar sweet pickles
1 can anchovy fillets
small can hot chilies
assorted breads
unflavored gelatin
small jar capers
1 pt heavy cream
4 oz sour cream

## Staples

parsley
garlic
Dijon mustard
flour
eggs
butter
onions

lemons
tarragon vinegar
olive oil
sugar
vegetable oil
tarragon
salt
pepper mill

peppercorns
bay leaf
Tabasco
coriander
thyme
mace
paprika

# Menu 29

This is my most popular informal buffet dinner and one that adapts nicely to large crowds. By increasing the recipes, you may easily serve many more than 10. A tray of crisp raw vegetables, a cheese board, and bowls of fresh fruit may be added. With about an hour advance preparation time, this buffet, including the arrangement of the table, can be prepared in about 2 hours.

## Planning Ahead

The first thing to be prepared on the day of the dinner is the pastry crust for the sausage. While it is chilling, assemble the strawberry bavarois and chill. After that, go right down the line, with the exception of the marinated mushrooms which should have been prepared at least 24 hours in advance. Serve the meats at room temperature, and chill the salads for serving. The entire buffet can be arranged on the table before the guests arrive. Dinner plates and cloth napkins wrapped around forks can be at one end of the table. If you have room on the buffet table, or perhaps on the table that serves as the bar, place an ice-filled bucket of splits of champagne, white wine, and bottles of beer for those not wishing hard liquor. An ice bucket, wine glasses, and bar glasses complete the arrangements. Your guests may now serve themselves.

# Broiled Herbed Chicken Legs

Prepare the following marinade: 1 cup vegetable oil, ½ cup lemon juice, 2 tablespoons minced tarragon, ¼ cup minced parsley, 2 crushed garlic cloves, ½ teaspoon salt, ½ teaspoon pepper.

An hour before broiling, pour the marinade over 10 chicken legs. Broil close to the flame, approximately 5–6 minutes each side. Drain marinade and serve chicken at room temperature.

### Food Processor Method

The marinade may be prepared in the processor using the steel knife.

# Sliced Roast Veal with Mustard Sauce

Select a 3-pound veal rib roast. Sprinkle with salt and pepper, spread with butter, and roast in a 350-degree oven 1½ hours or until the juices no longer run pink when the roast is pierced with a fork. Remove and allow to cool. Slice by the rib and arrange on a plate. Serve at room temperature with mustard sauce and paper chop frills at the tip of each chop.

## Mustard Sauce

Chop 3 small sour pickles, 1 small sweet pickle, and a teaspoon of tarragon. Blend with ½ cup prepared Dijon mustard and garnish with a little finely chopped pickle.

### Food Processor Method

With the steel knife in place, chop the pickles, add the tarragon and mustard.

# Sausage Baked in Pastry

Prepare the sour cream pastry on page 243, and chill. Prick a 1- to 1½-pound uncooked French or Italian sausage in 5 or 6 places to prevent the skin from bursting. Place in a deep skillet and add enough cold water to cover. Bring to a boil and simmer, covered, for about an hour. Drain and cool the sausage on paper towels, then split the skin with a sharp knife and peel it off. To wrap the sausage in crust, roll out the pastry to a thickness of about ⅛ inch. Cut dough to the shape shown in Figure 1.

Place sausage in the center of the dough, and gently lift the long sides of the pastry up over the sausage (Figure 2).

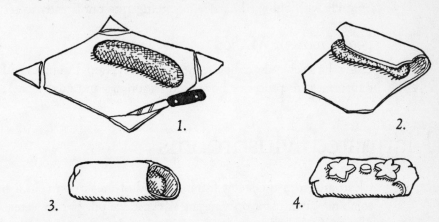

1.

2.

3.

4.

The pastry should overlap by about an inch; trim off anything more. Brush the edges with 1 egg beaten with a tablespoon of water and seal. Brush the ends of the roll with the egg and lift the flaps up and neatly seal (Figure 3).

Turn the wrapped sausage seam side down on a buttered baking sheet and decorate with the scraps of pastry dough cut into shapes (Figure 4).

Brush well with the rest of the egg mixture and bake at 375 degrees for 45 to 60 minutes until golden. Slice and serve with hot mustard.

### Food Processor Method

Prepare pastry in the processor, see page 244.

# Steak Tartare

For 10 people you will need about a pound of lean beef. Use top round, sirloin, or tenderloin. Trim any visible fat and grind meat just before blending. Mix into the meat in the following order: 6 well-chopped anchovy fillets, ¼ cup finely chopped onions, 1 tablespoon finely chopped chives, 1 egg yolk, 2 turns of the pepper mill, a dash of Tabasco, ½ teaspoon Dijon mustard, 1 tablespoon or more capers, 1 tablespoon cognac.

Be sure all the ingredients are well-blended. Taste for seasoning and add salt if necessary. Form into a loaf or a mound on a small bread board. Sprinkle with chopped parsley and refrigerate until ready to serve.

### Food Processor Method

Using the steel knife, chop the meat, remove, chop the chives and onions, return meat to processor bowl, add seasonings and mix, 1 or 2 seconds.

# Marinated Mushrooms

Clean and trim the stems from a pound of mushrooms. In a saucepan combine 1 cup tarragon vinegar, ⅓ cup olive oil, ¼ cup water, 4 sprigs parsley, 4 crushed peppercorns, 1 bay leaf, ½ teaspoon salt, and ¼ teaspoon each coriander and thyme. Bring the mixture to a boil and add the mushrooms. Simmer gently 2 minutes. Allow to marinate 24 hours. When ready to serve, drain and transfer the mushrooms to a serving dish and garnish with a little chopped parsley.

# Cucumbers in Sour Cream

Peel and remove the seeds of three large cucumbers. Slice thinly, place in a shallow dish and add half of a thinly sliced onion. Marinate for a few hours in lemon juice, salt and pepper. Pour off the juices and gently toss with sour cream, adding the cream a tablespoon at a time. Adjust the seasoning and decorate with parsley or any minced fresh green herb. Chill.

### Food Processor Method

Use the 2 mm slicing disc to slice the peeled and seeded cucumbers.

# Guacamole Salad

Mash the meat of 3 ripe avocados, reserving the pits. Mix with 1 large peeled, seeded, and chopped tomato, 2 or 3 tablespoons chopped canned chilies, 1 minced sweet green pepper, and 2 tablespoons minced onion. Add 2 tablespoons olive oil, 1 tablespoon lemon juice, a scant ½ teaspoon sugar, and salt and pepper to taste. Return the avocado pits to the mixture—this will keep the avocados green—and refrigerate until ready to serve. Remove the pits to serve.

## Food Processor Method

The tomatoes, chilies, green peppers and onions may be chopped in the processor using the steel knife. If the avocados are firm they may also be chopped in the machine.

# Assorted Breads and Toast

On a large tray arrange thinly sliced French bread, thinly sliced black bread and rye. On the same tray place several rows of white toast, homemade. Cover the breads with plastic wrap until ready to serve. Place plates of unsalted butter on either side of the bread tray.

# Strawberry Bavarois

Crush 4 cups of fresh strawberries and strain them through a fine sieve. Add 1 tablespoon lemon juice and ¾ cup sugar and stir until the sugar is completely dissolved. Soften 2 envelopes gelatin in ¼ cup cold water, dissolve it over hot water, and stir it into the purée. Fold in 2 cups stiffly whipped cream. Rinse a 2-quart mold in cold water, pour the strawberry cream into it, and chill thoroughly. This may also be prepared in individual molds. One-half hour before serving, unmold, garnish with whole berries, and return to the refrigerator until ready to serve.

# Menu 30

TO SERVE 12

Tapenado with Eggplant and Red Caviar Garnish

Marinated Artichokes

Galantine of Veal

Sliced Breast of Turkey

Assorted Breads

Coeur à la Crème

WINE
French or domestic
Pouilly-Fumé
or a fine Sparkling Rosé

## Shopping List

**Meat**
1 breast of veal, boned
bones from the veal
  breast
split veal knuckle
1 lb ground veal
½ lb smoked ham
½ lb ground pork
10-lb turkey,
  large-breasted

**Deli**
8 oz black olives
  (not tinned)

**Produce**
1 eggplant
assorted raw vegetables
  for tapenade
24 tiny artichokes
2 shallots
2 pt ripe strawberries
2 leeks
3 carrots

**Spirits**
cognac
dry white wine
Madeira wine

**Groceries**
4-oz can tuna
½-oz can anchovy
  filets
small jar capers
4 oz jar salmon roe
1 or 2 cans truffles
  (optional)
small can tomato paste
1 lb cottage cheese
1 lb cream cheese
1 pt heavy cream

## Staples

olive oil
lemons
tarragon vinegar
parsley
onions
garlic

chicken or
  veal stock
dry mustard
bay leaves
fennel seed
thyme

coriander
salt
peppercorns
allspice
marjoram
mace

# Menu 30

This is a more elegant buffet, though it is also slightly more complicated and time-consuming. It is designed to handle a lot of people easily at dinner. This menu also makes a lovely buffet lunch or a wonderful late evening buffet, where guests may not wish to eat too heavily.

## Planning Ahead

The tapenado and the turkey may be prepared the same day as the party. The galantine, marinated artichoke hearts, and coeur à la crème should be prepared at least 2 days ahead. Follow the method for the buffet arrangements on page 195.

# Tapenado with Eggplant and Red Caviar Garnish

Into the container of an electric blender, put 6 ounces pitted black olives, ½-ounce can flat anchovy filets, 4 ounces tuna fish, 2 tablespoons capers, 1 tablespoon cognac, 3 tablespoons olive oil, 1 generous teaspoon dry mustard, and freshly ground pepper. Start the blender and dribble in up to ¼ cup more olive oil and up to ¼ cup more cognac. As soon as everything is completely mixed and has the texture of a coarse, spreadable paste, stop the blending. Check the seasoning and texture. If the spread is too thick, add more olive oil; if flavor is not sharp enough, add more cognac and mustard.

### Food Processor Method

May be made entirely in the processor, using the steel knife.

## Red Caviar Garnish

Into the container of an electric blender put the juice of 1 lemon, 3 table-spoons olive oil, 4 ounces salmon roe, and 1½ tablespoons tomato paste. Blend at medium high speed. The consistency of the mixture should be that of a stiff mayonnaise. If it is not thick enough, add fresh bread crumbs, a tablespoon at a time. If too thick add more olive oil.

### Food Processor Method

May also be made entirely in the processor.

## Eggplant Garnish

Prick an eggplant with a fork in about a dozen places, rub with olive oil, and place in a baking dish in a preheated 400-degree oven. When the egg-plant is tender, about 1 hour, remove from the oven, cut open and dig out the pulp with a spoon. Put into a saucepan over medium heat. Mash down eggplant and stir continually to evaporate water and to thicken. Work in olive oil, spoon by spoon, the juice of a lemon, about a teaspoon of dried marjoram, plus salt and pepper to taste. When the mixture is about the consistency of mayonnaise, chill in the refrigerator. After it is chilled, check seasonings.

Arrange the tapenado with the 2 garnishes in separate dishes next to an attractively arranged platter of assorted raw vegetables. Some suggestions are cauliflowerets, carrot, celery, and zucchini sticks, radishes, etc. Serve plenty of thinly sliced French bread so that your guests may either dip the vegetables or spread the mixtures on the bread.

# Marinated Artichokes

Cut off the tips and pull off the tough outer leaves from 24 tiny artichokes. Cut in half through the stem and wash well. In a heavy saucepan, mix 2 tablespoons cold water, ½ cup olive oil, and ¼ cup tarragon vinegar. Bring to a boil and add 2 whole bay leaves, ¼ teaspoon fennel seed, ½ teaspoon each thyme and coriander, 1 teaspoon salt, 12 peppercorns, and 3 or 4 sprigs of parsley. Simmer covered for 5 minutes. Then drop in the artichoke hearts, making sure there is enough liquid to cover. If not, add more oil, vinegar, etc. Cover. Continue simmering gently until artichokes are cooked through. Let cool and refrigerate.

# Galantine of Veal

Have the butcher bone a breast of veal, reserving the bones. You will need a piece of meat about 12 inches long and 8 or 9 inches wide; it might be necessary to pound the meat to get the desired size. Lay the veal in a large container. Cut ½ pound smoked ham into ½-inch cubes and fit neatly around the veal. Sprinkle with salt, allspice, peppercorns, and, if desired, sliced truffles. Pour over ½ cup cognac and ½ cup Madeira wine. Cover tighly with foil and marinate about 5 hours. Grind finely ½ pound pork and 1 pound veal. Mix with ¼ cup chopped parsley, 2 minced shallots, ½ teaspoon salt and pepper. Refrigerate until ready to stuff the veal.

When ready to stuff, place the veal slab, wiped dry, on a large double-thick piece of cheesecloth. Strain the marinating liquid into the ground-meat mixture, add the marinated ham and truffles, and mix thoroughly. Place this stuffing down the center length of the veal slab, stopping about 2 inches from each end. Now roll up the veal carefully, wrap it tightly in cheesecloth, and tie it with string. It must be secure, as you do not want to lose the stuffing. Set the galantine in the bottom of a large heavy pot, pack around it the veal breast bones and a split veal knuckle. Add 2 leeks, 3 carrots, and 2 onions, all in chunks, 2 cloves of minced garlic, 2 teaspoons each marjoram and thyme, a few sprigs of parsley, 2 whole bay leaves, 12 whole peppercorns, ½ teaspoon mace, and ½ teaspoon salt. Pour in just enough chicken or veal stock and dry white wine to cover the galantine. Bring quickly to a boil, then turn heat down, cover, and simmer gently for 2 hours. Turn off the heat and let cool in the stock.

Lift out the galantine and set it on a platter to drain. Weight it while it cools. Strain the liquid from the pot and add ½ cup Madeira wine. This should cool into a firm jelly; if it is not quite firm enough, cook it more to reduce it. Finally, when the galantine is cool, remove the cheesecloth, place the galantine seam-side down in a mold, reheat the jelly, and pour over the galantine. Cover and refrigerate. Unmold and slice to serve.

### Food Processor Method

With the steel knife, chop the shallots and parsley, add the bacon and veal and chop, add seasonings and process.

# Sliced Breast of Turkey

Roast a 10-pound turkey according to your favorite method. Do not over-cook, as the turkey will be dry. Let stand at least 2 hours. Carve the breast meat and arrange attractively on a platter. Sprinkle generously with salt, pepper, and finely minced parsley.

# Assorted Breads

See page 199.

# Coeur à la Crème

Press a pound of cottage cheese through a fine sieve and combine with 1 pound cream cheese and 2 cups heavy cream. Beat until smooth and season to taste with salt. Line a large heart-shaped basket with cheesecloth and fill it with the cheese. Stand the basket on a plate in the refrigerator for two days to drain off the whey. When ready to serve, unmold onto a platter and garnish the *coeur* with strawberries that have been sprinkled with sugar. Individual heart molds may also be used.

## Food Processor Method

With the steel knife, process the cottage cheese until smooth, add the cream cheese and cream and continue to process until perfectly smooth.

# Slim Menus

# Menu 31
TO SERVE 6 TO 8

Fresh Clam and Tomato Soup

Grilled, Broiled or Sautéed
Fish Filets with a Slim Sauce

"Steam-Baked" Potatoes

Poached Pears in Fresh Raspberry Purée

WINE
*For reduced calories,*
*try mixing a sparkling water*
*with your favorite dry white wine.*

## Shopping List

**Fish**
3 doz clams
fresh fish filets
  (approx. 6 oz each)

**Produce**
carrots (3)
1 leek
shallots (2)
fresh herbs (parsley,
oregano, thyme, basil)
chives, mint
6 tomatoes
6 large, or 12 small,
  new potatoes
6 small, or 3 large,
  pears
2 baskets raspberries

**Groceries**
tomato purée (2 T)
1 pt lowfat ricotta
1 cup lowfat yoghurt

**Spirits**
1 bottle white wine

## Staples

vegetable oil
garlic
beef or chicken stock
  (6 cups) page 239

meat glaze (5 oz)
  page 240
fish glaze (1 oz)
  page 240

"slim cream" (4 oz)
  page 214
sugar

# Menu 31

In recent years there has been a great deal of interest in bodily fitness and good health. Because of the demand, we started a series of slim cooking menu classes, two of which I'm presenting here. Essentially what I have done is to reduce the fat content of the dishes without losing flavor or producing a dry or typical "diet" meal. I have served the following menus for company dinners without anyone being aware they were enjoying a "slim" menu.

## Planning Ahead

This entire menu may be prepared in advance. Hours ahead, poach the pears and let stand in the syrup to cool, purée the berries and place the sauce in an attractive serving dish. Pears may be placed on serving dishes before dinner and napped with sauce at serving time. Soup may be completed hours ahead and heated for serving. Fish may be cooked and set aside, sauce completed and heated to serve. Potatoes may also be finished and heated to serve (pages 8 and 9).

# Fresh Clam and Tomato Soup

Scrub 3 dozen live clams and steam them open with ½ cup white wine. Remove the clams from the shells and discard the shells. Strain out any sand from the clam broth and reserve both the clams and broth. Heat 1 tablespoon vegetable oil in a 6-quart pot and sauté 2 medium carrots, 1 leek, whites only, 2 shallots and 1 garlic clove (all coarsely chopped) for 5 minutes. Add a handful of chopped fresh herbs, (parsley, thyme, oregano, basil, etc.) 6 tomatoes, peeled, seeded and chopped, 2 tablespoons tomato purée, 6 cups homemade beef or chicken stock (page 239) and 2 ounces meat or chicken glaze (page 240) and simmer gently, covered, for 30 minutes. Add the reserved clam broth and simmer another 20 minutes uncovered. Taste and season with salt, pepper and a pinch of sugar. Add the steamed clams, being careful not to cook them any more, and garnish each serving with lots of freshly chopped parsley.

### Food Processor Method

All the vegetables may be chopped using the steel knife.

# Grilled, Broiled or Sautéed Fish Filets with a Slim Sauce

Simmer a carrot in water until tender, discard water and add 4 ounces white wine, 2 ounces of concentrated fish stock (page 240) and 3 ounces concentrated meat stock (page 239). Reduce the liquid by half. Add 6 ounces of "slim cream" (recipe following) and purée the sauce in a blender or food processor. Season to taste with salt and freshly ground pepper.

Select fresh fish filets, approximately 6 ounces per person, and grill, broil or sauté as desired, being careful not to overcook the fish—usually 40 seconds each side is adequate. Serve the filets on a bed of sauce, garnished with snipped chives.

# "Slim" Cream

Combine 1 pint lowfat ricotta cheese, 5 tablespoons lowfat yoghurt and a pinch of salt, blending in an electric blender until very smooth—about 1 minute. Store in the refrigerator overnight before using.

### Food Processor Method

This sauce may be made in the food processor.

# "Steam Baked" Potatoes

The following method of cooking potatoes is dependent upon a porous clay casserole, one that when soaked will absorb water and then, in a hot oven, will allow the vapor to surround the potatoes.

Scrub or peel 6 or 8 large, or 12 or 14 small, new red potatoes and soak in cold water for 20 minutes while your clay casserole soaks in warm water. Drain the casserole and place the potatoes in it whole, without drying them. Add salt, freshly ground pepper, 2 whole cloves of garlic and a generous handful of fresh herbs (parsley, thyme, marjoram, etc.) of your choice. Cover the casserole and place it in a cold oven. Turn the oven to 400 degrees and bake. Check for doneness with a wooden skewer in approximately 1 to 2 hours. Remove and discard garlic. Replace the cooked herbs with fresh ones to serve.

# Poached Pears in Fresh Raspberry Purée

Peel, halve and core 1 small pear or ½ a large pear for each serving. (Whole pears may be carved into "perfect" pear shapes at this point.) Poach the pears in a light wine syrup until tender, using a wooden skewer to check doneness. Allow the fruit to cool in the syrup.

## *Wine Syrup*

Combine 4 oz sugar in 1 cup white wine and 1 cup water. Bring to a boil and simmer 5 minutes before adding pears.

## *Berry Purée*

Purée 2 baskets of fresh berries in the blender or food processor with 2 tablespoons of poaching syrup from the pears. If desired, the berry seeds may be removed with a food mill or sieve.

To serve, place the pears in individual glass bowls and mask with the berry purée. Garnish with a few slivered, blanched almonds and a mint leaf.

## Food Processor Method

This purée may be done in the processor. The processor will not eliminate the seeds, however.

# Menu 32

TO SERVE 8

Spinach Salad

Filets of Chicken Breast with Lemon Sauce

Carrot Purée

Apples Filled with Fresh Fruit

WINE
*For reduced calories,
try mixing a sparkling water
with your favorite dry white wine.*

## Shopping List

**Poultry**
6 boned half-breasts
  of chicken

**Produce**
1½ lb spinach
10 mushrooms
3 lemons
1 bunch parsley
2 lb carrots
6 apples
2 baskets strawberries
½ lb cherries
1 peach
1 nectarine
2 plums, or equivalent
  fruits in season

**Spirits**
Sherry wine (1 cup)

**Groceries**
2 oz slivered almonds
8 oz lowfat yoghurt

## Staples

eggs (3)
red wine vinegar
Dijon mustard

9 oz meat glaze
  (page 240)
sugar

salt
pepper
"slim cream" (page 214)

# Menu 32

This menu is a visual delight as well as a medley of different textures, from the deep green of the leafy spinach salad to the succulent chicken breast with the colorful and velvety carrot purée to the firmness of the raw fruit served in the apple. A part of my slim cooking and eating philosophy is that appetite can be satisfied with food textures and food appearance. I think you will find, as we have, that you don't always have to eat rich, fatty food to feel satisfied!

## Planning Ahead

Hours ahead, have the spinach washed and crisping in the refrigerator, the mushrooms, cheese, chopped egg white and slivered almonds prepared next to a bowl of the "slim cream" dressing, ready to be tossed. Complete the chicken dish and leave it in the sauté pan to be heated (page 9). The purée may be completed and left in the pan to be heated and served. Have the fruit-filled apples on plates in the refrigerator, ready to be served at the table.

# Spinach Salad

Wash 1½ pounds of spinach, remove the stems, dry well and crisp in the refrigerator. Just before serving, place spinach in a large salad bowl. Add 2 ounces slivered, toasted almonds, 3 chopped hardcooked egg whites, and 10 thinly sliced mushrooms. Toss with the following sauce: Combine 1 cup slim cream (page 214), 1 ounce of red wine vinegar, 1 ounce of meat glaze (page 240), 1 tablespoon Dijon mustard, 1 teaspoon sugar, freshly ground salt and pepper to taste. Note: Begin by tossing salad with only 6 tablespoons of the dressing. Add more by the tablespoon if needed.

### Food Processor Method

The mushrooms can be sliced in the processor using the 2-mm slicing disc. The egg whites can be chopped using the knife, and the salad sauce mixes very nicely in the machine, again using the knife.

# Filets of Chicken Breast with Lemon Sauce

From your poultry man, select 8 half-breasts of chicken. Skin, bone and filet them (see note following). Pass the chicken fillets through flour, shake off any excess and sauté in a little oil 30 seconds each side. Season with salt and pepper and remove to a platter. Pour off any remaining fat in the pan and add 1 cup of meat glaze (page 240), the juice of one-half a lemon, and 1 cup good quality sherry wine. Simmer slowly until sauce is reduced and thickened (page 6). Taste and season with salt and freshly ground white pepper. Return filets to sauce for warming before serving (page 8). Garnish with chopped fresh parsley. Serve 3 filets per person.

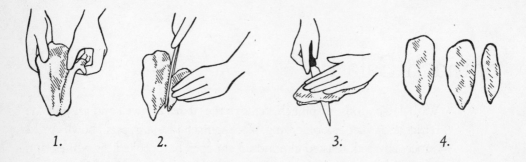

1.     2.     3.     4.

### Filleting a Boned and Skinned Chicken Breast

Begin with a skinned and boned half breast. On the underside of the breast, the part that was next to the bone, there is a smaller muscle that may easily be separated from the rest of the breast with your fingers (1). Finish cutting the piece off using a sharp knife (2). Lay the remaining larger piece of breast meat on a cutting board, and holding it flat with one hand, slice it into two filets (3). Three filets from one half breast (4).

# Carrot Purée

Boil 2 pounds of carrots in salted water until soft. Purée in the food processor or blender until perfectly smooth. Add 2 ounces slim cream (page 214) and continue to process until cream is incorporated into purée. If purée is still too thick, add a little more "cream" until it thins to the proper consistency. Season with salt and freshly ground white pepper. Warm slowly before serving.

## Food Processor Method

This purée may be made in the machine using the steel knife, leaving the processor on until the mixture is smooth.

# Apples Filled with Fresh Fruit

Wash 6 apples. Slice off the tops and reserve in a bowl sprinkled with lemon juice. With a melon baller, scoop out the meat of the apples, discarding the seeds and cores. Add the apple balls to the bowl of apple tops in lemon juice. Sprinkle insides of apples with lemon juice. Peel, slice or cut your choice of fruits in season (strawberries, peaches, cherries, etc.) into tiny dice. Fill each apple with the chopped fruits. Pour 2 tablespoons strawberry sauce over the fruit, and put on the caps. Set the apples in chilled glass dessert bowls, pour some strawberry sauce around them and decorate the tops with mint leaves.

### Food Processor Method

The fruit may be diced and the strawberries puréed (see following recipe) using the steel knife.

## Strawberry Sauce

Purée 1 pound of strawberries with 6 tablespoons sugar and the juice of half a lemon.

# Nouvelle Cuisine

# Menu 33
TO SERVE 6

## Cold Bay Scallops
with a Delicate Vinaigrette

## Salmon Filets
with a Sorrel Sauce

## Steamed Buttered Potatoes

## Kiwi Custard Tart

WINE
A Napa Valley Chardonay or
French Montrechet

## Shopping List

**Fish**
2½ lb scallops
6 salmon filets,
   approx. 6 oz each

**Produce**
6 small tomatoes
3 avocados
5 lemons
1 bunch parsley
shallots (4)
1 bunch sorrel
tiny new potatoes,
   allow 2–3 per person
6 kiwi fruit

**Spirits**
1 bottle white wine
cognac

**Groceries**
1 pt whipping cream
   *or* créme fraîche

## Staples

fish glaze
   (5 oz)
eggs (2)
flour

Dijon mustard
walnut oil
   (1 cup)
sugar

salt, white pepper
cayenne pepper
paprika
butter

# Menu 33

Often confused with "cuisine minceur," the new French cooking is not slim cookery. Based on the classic Escoffier style, some imaginative French chefs have changed the old style drastically. Simplicity of menu, preparation and flavors are now preferred. There is a lightness to the dishes, with less or no flour in the sauces and puff pastry favored. The garnishes are simpler and, most significant, there are shorter cooking times on all fish, vegetables, and meats. An awareness of health, exercise and nutrition pervades. This menu is my version of the nouvelle cuisine.

## Planning Ahead

Complete all preparation on the scallop salad in advance. Assemble salads on serving plates before the dinner guests arrive, and place them in the refrigerator until serving time. When ready to eat, place each salad on the dinner table and sprinkle with vinaigrette. Pass additional sauce. Complete preparation of salmon before guests arrive, leaving the fish separate from the sauce in a cool place. When ready to serve, gently warm the salmon in the sauce, not more than a minute, so as not to overcook. Steam potatoes in advance, transfer to a pot with butter, salt and pepper, to be warmed when ready to serve. The tart should be completed at least two hours before guests arrive.

# Cold Bay Scallops
## *with a Delicate Vinaigrette*

Clean carefully 2½ pounds bay scallops. Cut into smaller equal pieces and drop into rapidly boiling water for 30 seconds. Drain and place in a bowl. Sprinkle with vinaigrette and set aside. Peel and quarter 6 small ripe tomatoes. Peel and quarter 3 avocados, cut them into strips and sprinkle with lemon juice. When ready to serve, place a portion of scallops in the center of an attractive plate, and alternate the avocado and tomatoes around the scallops. Sprinkle with vinaigrette and finely chopped parsley.

## Walnut Oil Vinaigrette

Combine the following ingredients: 1 tablespoon minced shallots, 2 teaspoons Dijon mustard, 1 cup walnut oil, 5 tablespoons lemon juice, ½ teaspoon sugar, salt, and freshly ground white pepper to taste.

### Food Processor Method

The vinaigrette may be mixed in the machine using the steel knife.

# Salmon Filets
## with a Sorrel Sauce

Plan approximately 6 ounces of fish per person. Have your fishmonger bone and skin 6 salmon filets. Lightly flour the salmon filets and sauté in unsalted butter 30 seconds each side, transfer to a platter.

## Sorrel Sauce

Sauté 3 finely chopped shallots until softened but not colored. Pour off any remaining butter and add 5 ounces fish glaze (page 240) and 1 cup white wine and reduce the sauce by three-quarters. Add 1 cup sweet cream or crème fraîche (page 240) and reduce once again to a consistency of very thick cream. Season with salt, cayenne pepper, and paprika. Shred 2 handfuls washed sorrel, soften in a little butter and add to the sauce. When ready to serve, warm salmon fillets in sauce, place on plate and cover with sauce. Serve with steamed potatoes if desired.

## Food Processor Method

The shallots may be chopped in the machine using the steel knife.

# Kiwi Custard Tart

Roll out tart pastry 1 or 2 (page 244) and line an 11-inch tart mold. Chill 30 minutes, line with parchment paper, fill with pie weights and bake at 350 degrees until edges begin to brown—about 20 minutes. Remove paper and weights and bake 5 more minutes. Combine 2 whole eggs, 2 egg yolks, ¼ cup sugar (or to taste), 1 cup creme fraîche or sweet cream (page 240), and 2 tablespoons Cognac and stir well. Pass the custard through a fine strainer. Peel and slice 6 kiwi fruit. Arrange kiwis on the pre-baked pastry, pour the custard over all and bake at 350 degrees until barely set—approximately 20 to 30 minutes. Preheat broiler, sprinkle tart with sugar and place under flame to caramelize, approximately 1 minute.

## Food Processor Method

The tart pastry may be made in the machine (page 244) and if the kiwis are firm they may be sliced using the 4-mm slicing disc.

# Menu 34

TO SERVE 6

## Individual Fresh Tomato Soufflés

## Stuffed Chicken Breasts
with a Green Bean Sauce

## Walnut Ice Cream

WINE
*A Napa Valley Chardonay or
French Montrechet*

## Shopping List

**Meat**
6 half-breasts of
   chicken (boned)

**Produce**
6 lb tomatoes
1 carrot
1 shallot
5 medium mushrooms
1 leek
1 lb green beans
   (including 10 nicely
   shaped ones for
   garnish)
1 lb walnuts in the
   shell

**Spirits**
Port wine

**Groceries**
5 cups heavy cream
honey

## Staples

paprika
salt
white pepper
cayenne pepper

sugar
butter
eggs (14)
flour

milk (½ cup)
4 oz meat glaze
   (page 240)
vanilla extract

# Menu 34

This is an elegant menu for a small group of guests who understand and appreciate fine cookery. The fresh tomato soufflés at the beginning of the meal are a light and elegant contrast to the rich, velvety ice-cream dessert. The beautiful green color of the flourless sauce for the chicken is from the puréed green beans, a typical nouvelle cuisine sauce. Sliced potatoes sautéed in butter are a nice garnish. A simple butter lettuce and parsley salad is recommended before dessert.

## Planning Ahead

The tomato soufflés may be completely assembled in their individual dishes and refrigerated until ready to bake. They may go directly from the refrigerator into the oven and must be served immediately out of the oven. The chicken breasts may be completely finished and reheated to serve, being careful not to overcook. The ice cream should be finished and allowed to ripen in the freezer at least 2 hours before serving.

# Individual Fresh Tomato Soufflés

Peel, seed and dice 6 pounds of ripe tomatoes. Sprinkle with salt, pepper, and sugar. Heat 2 tablespoons butter in a sauté pan and add the tomatoes. Simmer gently until the liquid has evaporated. Adjust seasoning and pass through a food mill. Add ½ cup bechamel sauce and 4 lightly beaten egg yolks. Combine well, taste and adjust seasonings once again. Fold 6 stiffly beaten egg whites into the base, divide into 6 individual, buttered soufflé molds and bake in a 400-degree oven for 7 to 8 minutes, until nicely puffed and browned. Serve immediately.

## Béchamel Sauce

In a saucepan melt 2 tablespoons butter, add 3 tablespoons flour and stir over a medium heat 3 or 4 minutes. Add ½ cup milk and stir until sauce thickens. Season with salt and white pepper.

# Stuffed Chicken Breasts with a Green Bean Sauce

First make the stuffing. Melt 3 tablespoons butter in a small sauté pan. Add 1 medium carrot, peeled and finely chopped, and cook over medium heat for 3 minutes. Then add 1 shallot, finely chopped, and cook 2 minutes more. Add 5 medium mushrooms, finely chopped, and cook 5 minutes more. Season with salt and white pepper and allow to cool slightly. Bone and remove the skin from 6 half-breasts of chicken. With a knife, slice open each breast so that you will form a small pocket. Season each pocket with salt and pepper and place a little of the vegetable stuffing in each. If necessary, secure with a toothpick. Do not overstuff.

### Food Processor Method

All the vegetables for the stuffing may be chopped in the machine using the steel knife.

## Green Bean Sauce

In a large sauté pan, melt 2 teaspoons butter. Add the white part of a leek, chopped finely, 2 ounces good-quality port, and 4 ounces meat glaze (page 240). Place the 6 stuffed chicken breasts in the pan and simmer, covered, 3 minutes each side. Remove breasts to a platter and continue to cook the sauce slowly, covered, until the leek is very soft. Then remove the cover and gently reduce to about ½ cup liquid. Pass sauce through a food mill or fine strainer, rinse out sauté pan, return the puréed sauce to the pan and add 2 cups heavy cream and approximately ½ cup green bean purée (see following recipe). If sauce is too thin at this point reduce over medium heat until sauce thickens. Season carefully with salt, white pepper, paprika, and a dash of cayenne. When ready to serve, gently warm chicken in the sauce, being very careful not to overcook (page 11). Serve chicken in the center of the plate, cover with sauce and garnish with a few cooked julienned beans.

## Green Bean Purée

Boil 10 green beans, being careful to retain their green color (page 242). Drain, julienne, and set aside for garnishing the chicken breasts. Boil 1 pound of green beans until soft, purée first in a food processor or blender and then pass through a food mill. If the purée is watery, return to a saucepan and simmer over low heat until thickened.

# Walnut Ice Cream

Chop coarsely 5 ounces freshly shelled and toasted walnuts. Bring 3 cups cream to a boil, turn off the heat, add a dash of salt, 2 tablespoons of vanilla extract and the walnuts. Beat 8 egg yolks with ½ cup honey until light and fluffy. Beating constantly, pour hot cream over yolks and beat until cooled. Chill and freeze in an ice-cream freezer. Garnish each serving with some toasted walnuts.

## To Toast Walnuts

Spread walnuts out on a baking sheet and toast in a 350-degree oven about 10 minutes.

# Basic Recipes

# Basic Recipes

## Beef/Brown Stock

Brown 3 pounds beef bones and 3 pounds veal (preferably neck) bones in a 350-degree oven for 2 hours or until they have a nice brown color. Transfer the bones to a large soup or stock pot (12- or 16-quart), cover with cold water and bring slowly to the boil. With a skimming spoon, remove the surface scum. Add 1 carrot cut into 4 pieces, a handful of celery tops, a leek, an onion stuck with cloves, 6 or 7 sprigs of parsley, and a bouquet garni. Skim as necessary while the liquid returns to the boil. Turn the heat down as low as possible so that the stock simmers, then cover the pot leaving the lid askew and simmer 3 to 5 hours, depending on how strong you wish the stock. When the taste is strong enough, strain the finished stock through doubled cheesecloth and chill overnight. Remove the congealed fat from the top and store the stock in the refrigerator for 3 or 4 days, or in the freezer up to 6 months.

## Chicken/White Stock

Use the same ingredients and method as in beef/brown stock, incorporating the following changes: Substitute 3 pounds chicken bones for the beef bones and eliminate the browning of the bones.

# Fish Stock

2 lb white fish heads and bones
1 shallot
celery leaves
bouquet garni

1 onion
1 carrot
1 cup white wine
approx. 1½ qt cold water

Follow same method as chicken/white stock, cutting simmering time to approximately 1 or 2 hours.

# Glazes, Concentrates, Essences, Extracts

First make a meat, chicken or fish stock. Strain out bones and vegetables and chill. Remove all visible fat and reduce the stock to approximately one-tenth its original volume. The glaze will be thickened and shiny. Pour into containers, mark and store in the refrigerator or freezer.

# Créme Fraîche
*Cultured Cream*

Créme Fraîche is a cultured cream, in taste somewhere between sweet cream and sour cream. It is thicker than sweet cream and is used a great deal in sauces—eliminating the possibility of separating or curdling. It is best to purchase a packet of dry créme fraîche culture, available in kitchen shops or health food stores—wherever yoghurt cultures are sold—and follow package directions. If you cannot locate the culture, try the following method: Combine well 8 ounces heavy sweet cream and 4 ounces buttermilk in a small saucepan. Put over a very low flame, stirring constantly until mixture reaches 90°F on an instant-read thermometer. Transfer to a container and keep warm (approximately 90°F) for 8 hours. A yoghurt maker is ideal. Store in the refrigerator.

# Lettuce Salads

I like a lettuce salad served after the main course. It is refreshing, especially after a rich dinner, and seems to serve as a perfect transition to dessert. The lettuce salad served after the main course should be a combination of complementary lettuces with a light vinaigrette sauce. The following preparation is necessary for salad greens: Discard the outer damaged leaves and rinse the remainder in cold water. It is not necessary to wash the inner core of some lettuces. Dry the leaves very gently to avoid bruising; a rotary salad dryer is preferred. Refrigerate greens wrapped in a towel to crisp. A half-hour before your guests arrive, tear enough leaves to make small salads for each guest, and put into a large salad bowl. The bowl must be large enough to allow for tossing. Put the salad, bowl and all, back into the refrigerator to chill until ready to serve. When ready to serve, toss with the salad sauce at the dinner table or in the kitchen and serve immediately. Following are some recommended salad-green combinations:

Butter or limestone lettuce and minced parsley

Watercress and endive

Romaine and butter or limestone lettuce

Three-quarter limestone or butter lettuce and one-quarter spinach leaves

# Vinaigrette Sauce
*Salad Dressing*

The kind of oil used for vinaigrette sauce is a matter of personal taste. Sometimes a filbert or walnut oil is appropriate and other times an olive oil is preferred. Since the vinaigrette is such a simple sauce, it is imperative that the ingredients be of the best quality. There is a wide variety of vinegars, oils and mustards to choose from: red wine vinegar, sherry vinegar, champagne vinegar, and vinegars flavored with herbs, raspberries, or strawberries, to name just a few. Taste your oils, vinegars and mustards just as you taste your wines before serving them. A different-tasting vin-aigrette is produced each time a different oil, vinegar or mustard is used.

When tossing a salad, don't pour on too much dressing. Start with a small amount—you can always add more. Toss gently with two long-handled spoons or forks and taste a leaf in order to judge whether or not there is enough dressing coating the leaves.

## *Basic Sauce Vinaigrette*

To the following basic sauce you may add herbs, fresh or dried, parsley, cheese, egg yolks, tomatoes, cream, mustard, etc. Let the type green and the rest of the menu be your guide. A vinaigrette may be made in quan-tity and stored in the refrigerator.

5 tablespoons olive, walnut, or
    filbert oil
1–2 tablespoons vinegar of
    your choice
¼ teaspoon freshly ground
    pepper or to taste

¼ teaspoon salt or to taste
⅛ teaspoon sugar
¼ teaspoon imported mustard

Makes approximately 1 serving.

# Cooking Green Vegetables

Green vegetables must remain a beautiful, bright green when they are cooked. There are several ways to achieve this. The following method, adapted from the Paul Mayer method, is the one I prefer.

Since the following method depends upon a utensil that can be heated dry, be certain that the cookware you have may be safely used in this manner.

Wash, peel, shell or otherwise prepare your green vegetables for cook-ing. Turn on the heat full under the saucepan or sauté pan intended for

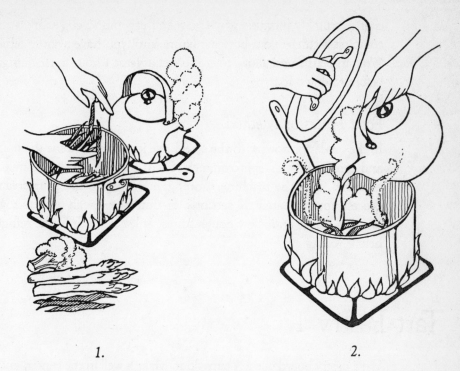

*1.*                    *2.*

the vegetables for a minute or two, in order to heat the container adequately so that when the boiling water is poured over the vegetables the water keeps boiling (Figure 1). In a separate teakettle or pot, bring to a boil an adequate amount of water to cover the vegetables. When the container for the vegetables is adequately heated, add the prepared vegetables, pour the rapidly boiling water over the vegetables, clap on a lid and check after 30 seconds for doneness. When the vegetables are done to your taste, drain, and finish the vegetables according to your recipe (Figure 2).

# Sour Cream Pastry

Combine 2¼ cups flour and 1 teaspoon salt in a large chilled bowl. Drop 6 ounces chilled unsalted butter, cut into ¼-inch bits, into the bowl. Working quickly, rub the flour and butter together until you have a coarse, crumbly mixture. Mix together 1 egg and ½ cup sour cream and combine with the flour-butter mixture until you have a soft pliable ball. Wrap in plastic and allow dough to rest at least 1 hour in the refrigerator before rolling out.

## Food Processor Method

In the processor bowl with the steel knife in place, combine the flour, salt and butter. Process approximately 8–10 seconds, until the mixture is crumbly. With the machine running, add the egg and sour cream and process approximately 30 seconds, or until the dough gathers together. Wrap in plastic and allow dough to rest at least 1 hour in the refrigerator before rolling out.

# Tart Pastry 1

On a pastry board pile 1¾ cups flour. Make a well in the center, and place in it 5 ounces chilled unsalted butter, cut into ¼-inch bits, ½ teaspoon vinegar or lemon juice, 2 tablespoons finely granulated sugar, a pinch of salt, and 2 egg yolks. With the tips of the fingers of one hand, quickly and lightly cream the butter, sugar, and egg yolks. Add ½ teaspoon ice water and blend flour into the creamed mixture until the dough gathers together. Wrap in plastic and allow dough to rest at least 1 hour in the refrigerator before rolling out.

## Food Processor Method

In the processor bowl with the steel knife in place, combine the flour, salt, sugar and butter. Process for approximately 8–10 seconds, until the mixture is crumbly. With the machine running, add the vinegar or lemon juice, egg yolks and water. Process until mixture gathers together, approximately 30 seconds. Wrap in plastic and allow dough to rest at least 1 hour in the refrigerator before rolling out.

# Tart Pastry 2

On a pastry board or in a bowl combine 2 cups unbleached flour, ½ teaspoon salt, and 5 ounces cubed unsalted chilled butter. With the tips of your fingers or a pastry cutter combine until mixture is coarse and crumbly. Add ½ teaspoon vinegar or lemon juice and enough ice water (start with 1 tablespoon) to cause dough to gather together. Wrap in plastic and allow dough to rest at least 1 hour in the refrigerator before rolling out.

## Food Processor Method

In the processor bowl with the steel knife in place, combine the flour, salt, and butter. Process for approximately 8–10 seconds until the mixture is combined and crumbly. With the machine running, add the lemon juice and ice water, processing until mixture gathers together, approximately 30 seconds. Wrap in plastic and allow dough to rest at least 1 hour in the refrigerator before rolling out.

# Tomato Sauce

Melt 1 tablespoon butter in a saucepan and add 1 clove of garlic which has been crushed through the garlic press, 1 small can of tomato paste, a 1-pound can of peeled Italian tomatoes, chopped coarsely, ½ teaspoon sugar, and salt, pepper, and basil to taste. Cook uncovered until thickened. For a perfectly smooth sauce, sieve or pass through a food mill.

# Soufflé Dish Preparation

Dessert soufflés require a "collar" or band of buttered wax paper tied around the dish extending above the rim to prevent the soufflé from spill-

ing over before it has a chance to set. This is done with dessert soufflés, as they are generally lighter in texture than savory soufflés, therefore rising more quickly and taking longer to set. Butter the soufflé dish well and sprinkle with sugar, tilting the dish to make sure the interior is well coated. Then cut a piece of wax paper that will go around the dish, fold it in half lengthwise and butter, but do not sugar, this collar. Arrange it around the soufflé dish, buttered side in, and tie with a single piece of kitchen string. This may be prepared several hours ahead.

# Crêpes

Put the following into the container of a blender or processor: 2 eggs and ¾ cup milk. Add ½ cup plus 1 tablespoon of flour, 1 teaspoon oil, and a pinch of salt. Combine in the blender or processor for a few seconds. Allow the resulting batter to stand an hour or more. When you are ready to make the crêpes, heat a crêpe pan, grease it with a little unsalted butter (this is only necessary for the first one), and pour in just enough batter to cover the bottom of the pan. If you pour in too much, just pour the batter back immediately, before it has time to set. The crêpes must be paper thin. Cook over a moderate flame until the bottom begins to brown and the top is dry. You may turn the crêpe over and barely brown the other side if you wish, although it is unnecessary. Stack the crêpes on a board and cover with a cloth. If they are not to be used within a few hours, they may be frozen. The above recipe makes about twelve 7-inch or sixteen 5-inch crêpes.

# Beurre Manié

Cream together, with your fingers, butter and flour in proportions of 1 teaspoon butter to 1 teaspoon flour. Be sure that the flour and butter are completely incorporated. If the beurre manié is not to be used immediately, roll into little balls and refrigerate, to be used as needed.

# Bouquet Garni

Bouquet garni is the French term for a bundle of vegetables and herbs of your own choice or as specified in the recipe, tied together with string for easy removal. If you use all dried herbs, tie them into a little bundle of cheesecloth. A fresh bouquet garni might include a small celery stalk with leaves, a sprig of parsley, a bay leaf, and a sprig of thyme. Use vegetables and herbs in bouquet garnis as desired or as specified.

# Clarified Butter

Melt any desired amount of unsalted butter slowly over low heat in a heavy saucepan. When the last of the butter is melted, remove from the heat and carefully skim off the foam with a spoon. Strain the pure yellow oil through a fine sieve into a container, being certain to leave all the milky residue in the bottom of the pan. This pure oil, or "clarified butter," may be stored in the freezer for months. Clarified butter is used to brown delicate meats such as veal, lamb, or chicken quickly over a very high heat. It will not burn.

# Approximate Equivalents

## Liquid

8 ounces equal 1 cup or ½ pint or ¼ liter or 250 milliliters
16 ounces equals 2 cups or a demiliter or 500 milliliters
32 ounces equal 1 quart or a liter or 1000 milliliters
2 tablespoons equal 1 ounce

## Dry Weight

1 ounce equals 30 grams
8 ounces equals 240 grams
16 ounces equals 1 pound or 480 grams
35 ounces equals 2 pounds, 3 ounces or 1 kilogram
a pinch or a dash equals slightly less than ⅛ teaspoon
3 teaspoons equal 1 tablespoon
4 tablespoons equal ¼ cup

## Miscellaneous

1 large lemon equals ¼ cup lemon juice
5 large eggs equal 1 cup
8 large egg whites equal 1 cup

## APPROXIMATE EQUIVALENTS

12–15 large egg yolks equal 1 cup

1 cup flour equals 5 ounces (140 grams)

2 cups grated cheese equals 8 oz (240 grams)

1 cup dry bread crumbs equal 3 oz (80 grams)

1 cup raisins equal 5 oz (140 grams)

1 cup whole strawberries equal 5 oz (140 grams)

1 cup long grain rice equals 7 oz (200 grams)

1 cup whole almonds equals 5 oz (140 grams)

1 cup dry white beans equals 7 oz (200 grams)

1 cup chopped raw carrots equals 4 oz (110 grams)

1 cup raw cucumber, peeled, seeded, and chopped equals 5 oz
(140 grams)

1 cup tightly packed brown sugar equals 7 oz (200 grams)

1 cup confectioners sugar equals 4 oz (110 grams)

1 cup white granulated sugar equals 7 oz (200 grams)

# Recipe Index

## Desserts